SPAIN

TIME-LIFE BOOKS/AMSTERDAM

COOKERY AROUND THE WORLD

SPAIN

CORNELIA ROSALES DE MOLINO

Recipe photographs: Foodphotography Eising

France

Galicia

Asturias

Canta-
bria

Basque
Country

Navarre

Andorra

La
Rioja

Léon

Old
Castile

Aragón

Catalonia

Portugal

Madrid

Extre-
madura

Castile-
La Mancha

Valencia

Balearic
Islands

Murcia

Andalucía

Canary
Islands

Morocco

Algeria

Morocco

CONTENTS

SPAIN: LAND OF FIESTAS

Spain conjures up images of sun, sea and colour; of the white Mediterranean beaches and the dusty ochre heartlands; of the snow-capped peaks of the Pyrenees and the orange groves of Valencia. Don Quixote, Carmen, flamenco, siestas and bullrings: these are facets of a distinctive culture that combines romance and spectacle, drama and ceremony, excitement and relaxation. At its heart lies an exuberant appetite for enjoying life, witnessed by a multitude of religious and secular fiestas. Processions and pilgrimages, fireworks and dancing celebrate anything from a successful harvest to Spain's 15th-century deliverance from its Moorish invaders.

A somewhat festive approach is also a characteristic of everyday life. Typically, for example, Spain keeps much later hours than other European countries: the evening meal is eaten at any time up to midnight. A lively group of people might gather round a table beneath an arbour outside a restaurant, their children romping about without anyone bothering to tell them to sit still.

Fiesta or otherwise, food and drink are central to Spanish life. A traditional day, for example, would begin with a rather meagre breakfast: no more than a cup of coffee and a few biscuits say, or a visit to a pavement café or a *churrería* for *churros*—long, crisp, hot fritters, forced through a pipe into boiling oil to fry. Lunch at home with the family, in contrast, would be a rather more sumptuous affair, starting around 2 pm and often continuing into the late afternoon.

Around 7 pm begins the time for *tapas*, a wide range of appetizers that are offered by bars for customers to nibble as they sip their sherry, wine or beer. These distinctive Spanish snacks help stave off hunger until the evening meal, which is rarely before 9 pm. Finally, it is back to the bar where the evening began to drink a strong coffee or a glass of brandy.

To a large extent, of course, the leisurely midday meal has now gone the way of the afternoon siesta. Office workers in Madrid are as accustomed as those elsewhere to grabbing a quick bite at lunchtime; families have less time to lavish on their daily meal. The culinary traditions endure, however. Weekends and feast days still follow time-honoured patterns, bringing together family and friends to enjoy authentic Spanish cuisine.

This book tells you how to make your own delicious Spanish meals at home. The first chapter is an introduction to the country, its widely varied regions and their corresponding local dishes, products and festivals. Then come authentic recipes from all over Spain for everything from *tapas* and soups to desserts and pastries, arranged in the sequence in which they are traditionally served. There are recommendations for wine, notes on some of the more important ingredients and, where necessary, step photographs to explain complex techniques.

A glossary defines some of the less common terms and ingredients used in Spanish cookery. And suggested menus allow you to combine dishes in authentic meals that will conjure up a flavour of Spain at your own table. As the Spanish say, *"Buen provecho"*.

A COUNTRY OF MANY LANDS

The Spanish traditionally speak of their land in the plural, as *Las Españas*, reflecting a diversity that embraces four languages and many regions, peoples and cultures. Culinary traditions share the same regional differences, reflecting Spain's location between Europe and Africa, its varied geography and its rich history.

The Iberian peninsula it dominates was described by the poet W.H. Auden as "A fragment nipped off hot Africa, soldered so crudely to inventive Europe." And, indeed, the baked red hills of the southern interior could be part of Africa; the lush green valleys of Galicia in the northwest might be in Ireland. Spanish cookery reflects this hybrid character: the sweet or spicy dishes of Andalucía echo the climate and tastes of North Africa, whilst the warming stews of the Atlantic coast conjure images of temperate Europe.

North and south are separated by an interior which is largely rugged and inhospitable—Spain is Europe's most mountainous country after Switzerland. The weather of the vast umber plateau at its heart, the Meseta, is described as "Three months of winter and nine months of hell." Around this tableland are the mountains, threaded by a few unnavigable rivers, which kept the regions isolated from each other— just as the Pyrenees kept Spain largely cut off from the rest of Europe.

Along with geography, Spanish cooking has been shaped by the history of the peninsula, which has long attracted conquerors. Ancient Greeks, Romans, Celts, Carthaginians and Phoenicians all left traces of their influence. But the greatest legacy is that of the Moors, the Muslim people from North Africa who ruled much of Spain from the eighth to the 13th century, and who were not finally defeated by the Spaniards until the 15th century. Citrus fruits, almonds and seasonings such as saffron and cumin are reminders of what they added to Spanish cuisine.

When Columbus discovered America in 1492, he heralded the arrival of Spain's *Siglo de oro*, or Golden Age, when spoils from the New World made the country rich and powerful. The explorers brought back a wealth of unknown spices, and Spain's new grandeur was reflected in culinary advances. This period saw the highpoint of Spanish *haute cuisine*: it set the standards throughout Europe, and other rulers often imported Spanish chefs.

It is regional cookery, however, that remains the heart of authentic Spanish cooking. Fish and seafood dominate the Atlantic coast; game and roast meats are the traditional fare of the centre; Valencia's paddy fields yield rice for paella. Local specialities make the most of local ingredients and traditions; together, they create a rich cuisine that reflects the many-faceted nature of a complex country.

In their Sunday best, the
men of the Galician
fishing village of
Malpica escort a statue
of their patron saint,
Nuestra Señora de
Carme (Our Lady of the
Sea), across the harbour.
The ceremony, held each
summer, is to ensure an
abundant catch from
these rich waters.

Galicia, Asturias and Cantabria

The soil and the sea dominate the
cuisine of "green Spain", so called
because of the fertility of its rain-
watered earth. The region has long
been attractive to settlers. Cave
paintings in Altamira in Cantabria and
Tito Bustillo in Asturias are the legacy
of inhabitants of some 15,000 years
ago. Around 1000 BC ancient Celts
overran what is now Galicia, in Spain's
far-flung northwestern corner. They
found a mild climate and a mist-
cloaked, hilly landscape that was
more reminiscent of their northern
homelands than of the arid Spanish
heartland or the Mediterranean coast.

Today it is covered with tiny fields,
stone walls and slate roofs. Every
square metre of available land,
including man-made terraces cut into
the slopes of the inland mountains, is
covered with strips of crops—corn,
potatoes, tomatoes and beans. Isolated

from the rest of Spain by rugged peaks,
the Galicians retain traces of their
origins: traditional dances here are
accompanied by the bagpipes, which
are unknown in the rest of Spain.

Asturias and Cantabria, too, are cut
off by the towering ranges of the
Cantabrian Cordilleras and the Picos
de Europa that run parallel to the
coast. Their spectacular scenery of
snow-capped peaks, deep gorges,
forested slopes and lush meadows is
reminiscent of the Alps.

The cows that graze on the lush
mountain pastures in summer provide
some of Spain's best veal, and their
creamy milk is used for such dishes as
the renowned Asturian rice pudding
and the thick corn porridge that is a
characteristic local breakfast. The
area also produces Spain's answer to
Roquefort cheese, the creamy, mild,
blue-veined Cabrales, wrapped in tree
leaves and ripened like Roquefort in
limestone caves.

Cereal crops are important here: all over Asturias and Galicia there are long narrow grain stores, or *hórreos*. Built on short stone stilts to protect their contents from rodents and damp, these distinctive buildings are usually topped with crosses, so that they resemble tiny churches.

Asturias is renowned for *fabada*, a warming stew of large white beans and smoked sausage, which provides an antidote to the long and rainy winters. Like other mountainous areas, the region produces fine pork and ham—even salmon and trout here might be prepared with the fat of smoked pork. The beans are also combined with rabbit, partridge or mussels to create unusual but flavoursome dishes.

The Atlantic Ocean offers a range of treasures, which are harvested by Spain's most important fishing industry. The wild granite shores of the Bay of Biscay yield abundant fish and shellfish for regional dishes, such as stuffed squid boiled in its own ink. A particular delicacy is *vieiras*, large, fleshy scallops weighing up to half a kilogram from the fjordlike inlets on Galicia's western coast called *rías*. (The fluted scallop shell was the traditional emblem of thousands of pilgrims on *El Camino de Santiago*, or Way of St. James. This ancient pilgrimage route across Europe ends in the Galician town of Santiago de Compostela, where the relics of the apostle are kept in a majestic cathedral.)

Vieiras are usually oven-baked in their shells with a crisp, herby crust. In contrast, Galicians prefer to sauté other shellfish in a little oil, so as to retain their intense saltwater flavour.

A favourite dessert is *Tocino de cielo*, a light and creamy egg pudding. Known all over Spain, it is served here doused with cider, the chief drink of Asturias. The province is ill-suited for raising vines, but the golden, slightly sparkling and rather strong cider is drunk with meals in place of wine, and is also used for cooking. It is found at its best in a *chigra* or cider house, drawn sparkling fresh straight from the barrel.

As befits a region where shellfish rule, the best wine in neighbouring Galicia is white: light, tangy Albariño goes wonderfully with fish and seafood. The authentic way to drink it is from traditional *conchas*, simple white china goblets, which can be found in the markets of towns such as La Coruña.

Festivals

In September, the town of Oviedo celebrates the Feast of St. Matthew with bullfights and processions of decorated floats. The highlight of the year at Santiago de Compostela is the week-long Festival of St. James, which begins on July 25 with a huge firework display in the cathedral square.

High spirits in a Galician farmer's wife show her joy at the harvest. Good crops are crucial for Galicia's many small, traditional farms.

The waters of the Atlantic lie deceptively still beyond the tiny harbour of Ea, near Guernica in the Basque Country. Long moles form a harbour to shelter boats during the Bay of Biscay's notorious storms.

The Basque Country and Navarre

The Basque Country—rich in natural ingredients and with a culture that traditionally places great emphasis on excellence in cookery—is sometimes reckoned to be home to Spain's best cuisine. Hilly, green, damp and wooded, this is a well-farmed region of orchards and lush cattle pastures. Blinding fogs sweep suddenly south off the Bay of Biscay to cloak the land in mist; equally suddenly, the gloom is broken by the sun. The region is in part densely populated, especially round such industrial centres as Bilbao and Vitoria.

Neighbouring Navarre, dominated in the north by the lonely peaks of the Pyrenees and in the south running down to foothills and steppes, is also home to members of the ancient Basque race; others live on the far side of the Pyrenees in France. The different groups of this fiercely independent people are united by a unique culture, and by Euskera, their shared language, unrelated to any other known tongue.

The mountain streams of Navarre are full of firm-fleshed salmon and the trout that go to make the renowned *Truchas a la navarra*, whole trout stuffed with serrano ham and pan fried. Nearer the coast, people prefer their fish and shellfish from the cold, blue-grey waters of the Bay of Biscay. Among the most popular ways of preparing fish are *a la vasca* (Basque-style), with wine and green vegetables and *a la vizcaina* (Vizcaya-style) with a combination of sweet and hot peppers.

Mild sweet peppers are also an important ingredient in the traditional *Piperrada*, a colourful omelette in which they are combined with ham. Another characteristic local vegetable is thick, succulent asparagus. The inland woods harbour wild boar, hare, rabbit and all kinds of game birds.

As well as their fish dishes, Basque cooks are famous for sauces. Among the most delicious are the garlicky *pil-pil*, or the green *salsa verde* made with peas and flavoured with parsley. Other sauces often offer very distinctive flavours, containing unusual ingredients such as cinnamon or plain chocolate.

The local cheese is mild, buttery *Idiázabal* made from ewe's milk, which has a delicate, smoky flavour and is

Built for convenience right to the water's edge, traditional houses line the harbour of the small fishing village of Pasajes de San Juan, in the Basque province of Guipúzcoa.

often served with nuts or used for cakes and desserts. Sweets from the region include *pastillas*, delicious caramels from Pamplona, and chocolate truffles from Vitoria.

As for wine, a delicate red Alavesa, from the most northerly part of the Rioja wine-growing area, is light enough to be drunk throughout a meal. Better with fish, perhaps, is the Basque Chacolí, which is tangy and slightly sparkling. Pacharán, a fruity sloe liqueur, served ice cold, is a delightful finishing touch to a meal, as reflected in the popularity it has found recently all over the rest of Spain.

The traditions of local cuisine are preserved in special gastronomic societies that raise food to the level of a Basque national sport. Entirely male, they have their own club-houses where members meet regularly to try out new recipes and test the results. The high spot of the culinary year is the annual banquet of the gastronomic societies in San Sebastián on the evening of January 19, to which non-members are also welcome. Celebrations continue the next day, the feast of the town's patron saint, when to the beat of drums, processions of bakers and cooks make their way through the streets and until late into the night the city becomes a gourmet's paradise.

Festivals

The most famous and exhilarating of the region's festivals is the San Fermín fiesta in Pamplona in July, where young men dressed in white, with scarlet berets and scarves, run bulls through the streets. The human participants are traditionally allowed only a rolled-up newspaper to defend themselves with.

Massive sandstone outcrops of the Pyrenees tower over the village of Riglos. The bizarre formations of the soft rock are the results of millennia of erosion by the wind and rain.

A fisherman mends his nets in the busy port of Palamós on the Costa Brava. The so-called "wild coast" stretches north from Barcelona to the French border.

Catalonia

For many of the tourists who visit the Costa Brava in large numbers every year Catalonia is package holiday Spain, but this historic region has much more to offer. Behind the warm, subtropical coast, where palm trees and citrus fruits flourish, lie rugged mountains that cut the region off from the rest of Spain. Historically, Catalonia has been more closely tied to southern France than to the Spanish heartland; the Catalan language, mother tongue of five million people, resembles the old *langue d'oc* of France more than Castilian Spanish.

Isolation has fostered a distinctive and independent Catalan culture, celebrated by artists such as Salvador Dalí and Joan Miró, and by the architect Antonio Gaudí whose Art Nouveau buildings characterize the regional capital of Barcelona.

The city is home to one of the most characteristic celebrations of Catalan culture. On Sunday mornings scores of people gather outside the Cathedral of Santa Eulalia and join hands to perform the *sardana*, a traditional dance accompanied by wind instruments and small drums. The natural riches that are the basis of Catalan cooking come together in Barcelona's magnificent Art Nouveau market hall at La Boquería, grouped by colour in mouth-watering displays. There are olives, fruits and vegetables; sardines and monkfish freshly caught by the fishing fleet; wild autumn mushrooms called *rovellons*—a prized Catalan delicacy; and partridge, quail and wild hare brought in by hunters from the region's heart.

Catalonia is a land of geographical contrasts: to the north of Barcelona is the Costa Brava, or "wild" coast, with rocky cliffs and small inlets, while to the south of the city lie the long, golden beaches of the Costa Dorada; the slopes of the Pyrenees are thickly timbered but the flatter land below is heavily cultivated with grain, vines, olives, fruits and vegetables.

Contrast also characterizes Catalan cuisine. At its heart is a thrifty waste-not, want-not attitude plus a creativity that can result in unusual combinations of ingredients. The so-called "land and sea" dishes, for example, combine meat and seafood most other cooks would keep strictly separate: chicken and lobster in a hazelnut sauce, say, or rabbit with squid and prawns.

Of the many imaginative fish dishes

A market in Barcelona provides a colourful display of Catalonia's abundant vegetables, fruit, fish and meat.

of the coast, the most renowned is *zarzuela*. In this so-called "operetta" of seafood, a variety of fish and shellfish are bound in a stew by a subtle sauce of wine, tomatoes and saffron, which enhances rather than overwhelms the distinctive flavour of each fish.

Sauces are an important element in Catalan cooking, and are often hotter and more spicy here than elsewhere in Spain. *Romesco*, made from cayenne pepper or paprika, oil, almonds and sometimes tomatoes, goes equally well with grilled fish or meat. S*amfaina* is a thick and spicy vegetable sauce similar to *ratatouille*; it too can accompany meat or fish, but goes particularly well with poultry.

The classic Catalan dessert is *crema catalana*. This is a rich but light egg and milk custard resembling *crème brûlée*, with a thin crust of caramelized sugar traditionally crystallized with a special red-hot iron just before serving.

A suitable drink to accompany the region's savoury specialities is a dry Catalonian white wine; those from Penedés, just south of Barcelona, are particularly fine, as are those from Alella, which also produces smooth reds. Catalonia, and especially Sant Sadurní de Noya, is the centre for the production of Cava, the name given to sparkling white wines made by the champagne method; though differing in taste, they make a good alternative.

Festivals

In Barcelona, the Midsummer's Eve celebrations on June 23 centre around a huge bonfire on Montjuic, the hill that overlooks the port. Also in the city, the festival of Our Lady of Mercy, from September 24 to 28, is an occasion for bullfighting, folk dancing and a music festival. Around the same time, further down the coast in the town of Tarragona, the feast of St. Thecla is marked by folk dances and human pyramid contests.

Brightly coloured mosaic covers the 20-metre-tall "Dona i Ocell"–Woman and Bird–a sculpture by Joan Miró in a Barcelona park. Miró, a world renowned 20th-century Catalan artist, is held in special esteem in the city where he was born.

In traditional finery, women in La Alberca celebrate the feast of the Assumption with a mystery play. Such plays have been performed since medieval times all over Europe.

Soft sunshine falls on the 16th-century cloister of the convent of Las Dueñas in Salamanca, and the cathedral beyond. Since 1218, the city has been home to one of Spain's finest universities.

Old Castile and León

Old Castile and León are the historic heart of Spain. These are regions of endless horizons, with villages scattered among plains of wheat and rye in the north and farms of sheep and fighting bulls in the south. The earth is dry and cracked either by ice or heat all year round.

In contrast to the desolation of the unpopulated tracts of the Meseta plateau are the glories of the cities, which recall a rich past: walled Avila, Spain's highest and coldest provincial capital, for example; or Segovia with its fairy-tale castle and the world's finest working Roman aqueduct. The warrior El Cid, hero of the campaign against the Moors, is buried in Gothic Burgos, while Plaza Mayor in Salamanca, a medieval city of spires and domes, is one of the finest squares in all Spain.

Like the cities, the cuisine has the flavour of a bygone age. It is hearty and sustaining, a fortification against the brutal elements of land and sky. Meals often consist of roast meat cooked in old bakers' ovens over a wood fire of gorse, thyme or vine to impart a special herbal flavour. Baby lamb and suckling pig are killed much younger than elsewhere in Europe, making them very tender: "You can cut them with the edge of a plate," a saying goes. Waiters and cooks sometimes still do this, revealing juicy, light-coloured flesh beneath the crisp, dry skin. In the many restaurants based in old castles or monasteries, lit by torches or candles, such dishes are in perfect keeping with the medieval atmosphere.

Accompaniments for the copious meat are as simple as the roasts. There is the much-loved Spanish omelette called *tortilla*, served either as a plain potato omelette or in a gourmet version with green asparagus, tender ham or even prawns. Pulses—beans of all shapes and colours, used both fresh

Perfectly preserved, the walls that surround Avila in Castile are as forbidding today as in the 11th century when they were built to protect the city from the Moors. The walls—2.5 kilometres long, 12 metres high and three metres thick—incorporate 88 towers and nine fortified gates.

and dried, and *garbanzos*, or chick-peas—are also frequently featured. Served all over Spain, they are essential to Castilian cuisine, where they are the basis of the many versions of the stew-like *cocido*. They are also eaten boiled, or roasted and salted to make a tasty snack, sold by the bag at every street festival or fair.

The speciality of the city of León is a highly seasoned, creamy garlic soup. During the festival of St. Peter and St. Paul, in late July, it is cooked in huge cauldrons in the market square and served free to revellers.

Another local celebration is "trout week". To the north of the region rise the Cantabrian mountains, whose rivers and streams yield what are reputed to be the best trout in all Spain. Every August, León celebrates with angling competitions, cookery demonstrations and great feasts where trout are eaten "fisherman-style"—packed in clay and baked in the embers of an open fire.

A favourite treat is *yemas*, golden-yellow sweets made from egg yolks. The best come from Avila and make a delicious souvenir.

Either side of Valladolid are the thriving wine-growing areas of Rueda and La Ribera del Duero. Rueda, known for its sherry-like wines, now also produces refreshing, tangy whites; La Ribera del Duero's dry reds have a velvety quality. Other regional wines include the fruity reds from El Bierzo north of León and the heavier, dark reds of the Toro area further south.

Festivals

Segovians enjoy a reputation for gaiety, exemplified each February by the festival of Santa Agüeda, when women in traditional costumes take over the running of the province's villages. At the end of June, the city celebrates the feast of St. John and St. Peter with folk dancing and medieval ballads.

The holiday village of Torla is dominated by the towering outcrops of the Pyrenees. Torla lies at the entrance of Ordesa y Monte Perdido, one of Spain's finest national parks, and is a popular base for hikers.

Aragón and La Rioja

Aragón, whose northern border lies among the high peaks of the Pyrenees, was once a powerful medieval kingdom whose dominion stretched as far as Naples and the island of Sicily. The Moorish architecture of Zaragoza, the former capital, reflects a history of conflict and domination. The city stands in the midst of lush orchards and market gardens, but the appearance of fertility is deceptive. Only large-scale irrigation, with canals fed by the Ebro and other rivers, has made the one-time desert land arable.

Beyond the valleys lie the bleak, thinly populated plains of the Meseta plateau. Northwest of Aragón, La Rioja, Spain's premiere wine district, has a bare highland feel, with vineyards, crops and pasture alternating on the stony ground.

This harsh land has its own natural treasures. The emphasis here is on game: in the Pyrenees the mountain streams are full of fish, especially trout, and there are rich game reserves on the densely wooded slopes. As in other mountainous areas, sheep, goats and pigs are the characteristic domestic animals. La Rioja is the home of *chorizo,* a traditional smoked sausage which is renowned throughout Spain.

In general, the cuisine is hearty rather than refined. Trout are usually cooked quite simply, either fried or grilled; before cooking, however, they may be stuffed with ham, which makes them remarkably tasty. Lamb, kid and game are combined with aromatic herbs in the versatile shepherd's stew known as *Cordero a la pastora.*

In contrast, finely blended sauces are the basis of many dishes in Aragón, which belongs to the so-called *"zona de los chilindrones". Chilindrón* is the name of both a card game and a popular local sauce, though there is no clear connection between the two. The sauce, a pungent, slowly simmering blend of tomatoes, onions, garlic and sweet red peppers, with added ingredients such as *serrano* ham, chili peppers or saffron, suits practically any kind of meat, from tender little pigeons to heavy mutton.

The accompaniment to such dishes, essential for mopping up the sauce, is *migas*. These crisply roasted dice of garlic bread—resembling croûtons—are the colour of rust and are flavoured with sweet or hot pepper, or sometimes ham. Said to constitute the most ancient dish in the whole Iberian peninsula, *migas* are eaten everywhere in Spain, at any time of day, and with anything from meat sauces and fried vegetables to fruit and chocolate. The best bread for making them is the typical round, flat loaves baked in the wood-burning ovens or *panaderías* of small-town bakeries.

Zaragoza is famous for all kinds of mouth-watering cakes and pastries and for a range of tempting confectionery such as bitter-sweet marzipan.

The best accompaniment to any meal is a local wine: in Aragón, for example, the potent, dark red, violet-scented Cariñena. The centre of the region's wine production, however—and of all Spain—is La Rioja, the land along the Ebro River northwest of Aragón. Its vintages are often compared with those of Bordeaux, and its present high quality and worldwide reputation owes much to French winemakers who came here from Bordeaux in the 19th century to escape the phylloxera pest that was attacking their own vines.

La Rioja, though possessing a more upland character than the French were used to—the best vineyards are 450 metres above sea level—provided good growing conditions. Low vines flourished in a climate that was more benign than in much of Spain, with plentiful rain and relatively short summers and winters. Before the French eventually returned home, they had established their wine-growing traditions and expertise, which were previously lacking in Spain.

The main growing area is centred around the town of Haro. The finest Rioja wines are soft, fruity reds with a taste of oak from the Rioja Alavesa, which are lighter in colour than most Spanish wines; light reds (formerly called Claretes) are drier and lighter bodied. Of the white Riojas, the dry ones are crisp and lively, and generally better than sweet types.

Festivals

In October, the town of Zaragoza stages the Pilar Festival in honour of the Virgin of Pilar, patron saint of all Spain, with processions of giant lanterns borne through the streets on wagons, dance displays and bullfights.

The tranquil Río Oja, a tributary of the Ebro, runs along the western border of La Rioja, the region to which it gave its name.

Their faces tanned by outdoor working, three wine growers gather in the village of Pesquera, which lies in the south of the Rioja region.

Under the watchful eyes of trophy bulls, customers relax in a Madrid bar, famous for its tapas. A bloodsport with ancient origins, bullfighting still flourishes in Spain.

Madrid's 18th-century Palacio Real, or Royal Palace, was built by Philip V on the site of the city's old Moorish fortress, which burnt down in 1734.

Castile-La Mancha and Madrid

The high, umber-coloured plateau of the Meseta is a Romantic land where the spirit of Don Quixote still rides. Cervantes' knight-errant and his servant Sancho Panza shared their adventures in a 17th-century landscape much like that of today: fields of grain stretch as far as the eye can see; vines and thousands of hectares of lavender and purple-flowering saffron cover the plains; avenues of almond trees lead to scattered, clay-coloured villages. The idealistic knight famously jousted with the dazzling white windmills that still dot the landscape.

The autumn saffron harvest—Spain produces 70 per cent of the world's supply of this most highly prized spice, which until recently cost more per kilogram than gold—is celebrated by the election of a Saffron Queen, named for the damsel of Don Quixote's dreams, Dulcinea de la Mancha. The historic towns and buildings of the region—Aranjuez, the royal summer residence; aristocratic Toledo; the

monumental palace of El Escorial—recall the same age of chivalry.

Madrid, in contrast, is a relatively modern city. When it became Spain's capital in the 16th century it was a small provincial town; only within the last 200 years has it reached anything like its present size. It is a sprawling and vibrant capital—the highest in Europe—whose streets and squares bustle with life until late at night. The *Madrileños*, as the inhabitants are called, are renowned for an easy-going life style. It is said that the city has more than 8,000 bars, most of them full at all hours of the day and night.

The contrast of countryside and city is reflected in the cuisine. Madrid is also Spain's gastronomic capital, a melting pot where all the regional cuisines are available. The city stands amid virtual desert, and produce from all over the country is transported to its markets early every morning. The range of food available is remarkable, whether in the most expensive restaurants or the tiniest bars. Madrid is one of the few places in the heart of Spain where fresh seafood is common, for example. During the early evening, customers enjoying *tapas* scatter their prawn shells over the floor of the bar.

The main meal in the capital is traditionally eaten at lunchtime. It might begin with a salad or *Sopa de ajo*—garlic soup—and go on to a meat or fish course; or it might be a *Cocido madrileño*, the capital's version of a traditional Spanish dish. This slow-simmering casserole of meats, sausage, chick-peas and vegetables is eaten in separate courses: first the broth, then the meat, and finally the vegetables.

The food of La Mancha is substantial

rather than sophisticated, and based on the ingredients to hand. This area is known as the *tierra de pan*—the land of bread—because of its vast grain fields. The typical large, flat loaves are eaten with such dishes as *Pisto manchego*, a vegetable stew traditionally made with pork fat. Toledo is renowned for its partridges; the bird may be served spiced with cinnamon and cloves or marinated in a mixture of seasonings and served cold. The city is also famous for its marzipan.

There is a range of other specialities. The sheep of the central plains yield the milk that goes to make the tangy *queso manchego*, the most popular of all Spanish cheeses. Stamped with a flower as a mark of quality, it is also characterized by the corded pattern left on the rind by the hemp string that binds the cheese as it matures.

The plains of La Mancha are one of the largest wine-producing areas of Spain, but the wine, like the food, tends to be simple. In recent years, though some superior wines have emerged. The town of Valdepeñas gives its name to mainly soft reds, which are drunk as everyday table wine throughout Spain.

Festivals

For a fortnight in May, Madrid stages a huge fiesta of fireworks, bullfights and concerts in honour of San Isidro Labrador, the city's patron saint. In contrast, Toledo marks Corpus Christi with a solemn procession.

Symbols of peace and war, whitewashed windmills and a ruined 12th-century castle stand on a hilltop above the little town of Consuegra. The windmills, part of a group of seven, are used throughout the region to grind grain.

Toledo's spires are reminiscent of the works of one of its most famous citizens, the 16th-century painter El Greco. Spain's ancient capital has been declared a national monument, a testimony to its beauty and glittering past.

The monastery of Guadalupe is home to a "miraculous" image of the Virgin Mary, reputedly carved by St. Luke. Founded in 1340 by King Alfonso XI in thanks for a victory over the Moors, the monastery became a centre of learning and pilgrimage, and grew rich on tributes from the conquistadors.

Extremadura

The people of Extremadura call their region "Land of the conquistadors, land of the gods." From here came about a third of the conquerors of the New World, including Hernán Cortés, colonizer of Mexico, and Francisco Pizarro who conquered Peru. Those who returned built the ornate palaces that dignify many Extremaduran towns. But this proud history had its roots in poverty and emigration. The dry plains and hills of this vast, arid region, which is cut off from the rest of Spain by high sierras to the north and south, and borders on Portugal to the west, have long been unable to feed its population. The name itself comes from the Latin *terra extrema et dura*—a harsh, extreme land. Even today, it remains sparsely populated and unvisited.

Many of those who do visit head for Guadalupe, a centre of pilgrimage since the 14th century. The Guadalupe Virgin—a small, black-faced cedar statue—was reputedly carved by St. Luke. The conquistadors carried the fame of "the patron of all Spanish lands" throughout the New World.

Religion figures prominently in Extremaduran history and, more surprisingly, its cuisine. Its isolated monasteries are centres of retreat. That at Yuste, for example, was home to King Charles V for the year before his death in 1558, when he withdrew from the cares of this world to think about the next. In the monastic kitchens, which often provided hospitality for noble or royal guests, many outstanding recipes are said to have originated. One story claims that a cookery book smuggled out from one of them inspired French *haute cuisine*; another, that a French soldier, probably in Napoleon's army, declared that Extremaduran cooking made the invasion of Spain worthwhile.

Like other harsh lands, Extremadura depends on hardy animals and plants for its staples, and makes the most of little. Among the cork oaks, pines and chestnuts of the woodlands, pigs forage for acorns and chestnuts. Their meat is the source of delicate, air-dried hams such as that from Montánchez, near the regional capital Cáceres. *Morcón extremeño*, a sausage famed throughout Spain, varies in flavour from slightly sweet to hot as chili; it comes in a wide range of shapes.

The forests constitute one of Spain's most important game reserves, yielding deer, hare and game birds. "Take the sun from the hare and rabbit, and the shade from the partridge," says a hunter's proverb, referring to the animals' best meat: the saddle in one case, the breast in the other. The pheasant and partridge appear on local menus combined with truffles, another speciality: black winter truffles or *criadillas de tierra*, a pale, spotted truffle unique to Extremadura.

The cattle and sheep that graze on pastures bright with wild flowers

provide meat for other dishes. When the animals move north to the cool mountains in the summer an eerie emptiness falls over the land. Wild thyme and eucalyptus scent the air; in the south, slender wild asparagus is common. In the sun-soaked river valleys grow vegetables and fresh fruits, the region's favourite dessert.

Extremadura, though not a major wine-producing area, has some respectable table wines, including fresh white Almendralejo and the sherry-like whites from Cañamero, which are among the world's strongest unfortified wines. Of the reds, the meaty Lar de Barros is an excellent choice.

Festivals

Every October, Guadalupe celebrates the discovery of America, because it was there that Columbus received the king's permission to sail on his voyage. Many Extremaduran pigs are dedicated to St. Anthony, and his feast day in January is marked by a slaughter of mature hogs and the blessing of piglets by sprinkling them with holy water.

Women dance in Trujillo's Plaza Mayor, one of Spain's finest squares. Little more than a village in size, Trujillo is full of grand architecture, legacy of the riches sent home by the conquistadors.

The Levante: Murcia and Valencia

To the Moors who settled here 1,200 years ago, the Levante seemed a heaven on earth. Today it still enjoys the blessings of a mild Mediterranean climate, plentiful sunshine and rich soil. The Levante—the name means "land of the sunrise", or the East—is Spain's market garden: the plain around the city of Valencia can produce three or four vegetable harvests a year. This plenty is not entirely natural, however. To counter low rainfall, the Romans built irrigation canals, which were later improved by the Moors.

Moorish influence is also visible in the Arabian appearance of the villages scattered along the Costa Blanca, or white coast, named for the colour of its sand. To the north lies the Costa del Ahazar—the orange blossom coast—where in the evenings the white blossom fills the air with its perfume.

The region is Spain's *zona de los arroces*—land of the rice. The emerald-green paddy fields around the Albufera lagoon produce rice for many regional specialities, including the Levante's best-known dish and the most famous in Spain: paella. *Paella valenciana,* the local version, can vary enormously. At its simplest—rice and a few fish—it shows its origins as a dish of the poor; the most lavish version, on the other hand, contains many different kinds of meat, fish and vegetables, luxuriously garnished with crayfish. Whatever the ingredients, paella should be cooked in and eaten from the two-handled pan after which it is named; traditionally, too, it is eaten only at lunchtime.

The wide choice of fish and shellfish is not used only for paella. There are fresh anchovies, also served as *tapas* marinated in vinegar—the popular *Boquerones en vinagre*—and grey mullet, whose roe is as expensive and exquisite as caviar. Lake Albufeira, famous for its eels, also lends its name to a garlic and almond sauce eaten with fish. It was the Moors who introduced almond trees to the region, and the nuts are the basis of many almond and marzipan sweets and pastries. The most famous, *turrón*, is a nougat made in Alicante from toasted almonds, honey and egg whites.

The most important legacy of the invaders, however, remains the irrigated market gardens of Valencia, called *huertas.* They provide peppers, tomatoes, onions, artichokes and asparagus, best tasted in, for example, the fresh, crisp *ensalada mixta* that accompanies most meals in the region. In Murcia, the Moorish influence is shown in dishes of sweet roasted peppers and tomatoes. Another local speciality is *tronchón,* a creamy ewe's

Where the hills meet the coastal plain just south of Valencia lie the paddy fields of the Levante. Here is grown virtually all of Spain's rice.

milk cheese made in rounds with a funnel-shaped hollow on the sides.

Citrus and pomegranate trees line the roads and canals, and vines flourish in the sun. The Levante is one of Spain's major producers of table wines. Vineyards are concentrated largely around Valencia, from where come some of the region's best wines, Utiel-Requeña and Alicante. Perhaps the most characteristic drink, however, is sangría, Spain's famous punch of red wine and citrus fruits, which captures the Levante's sunny character.

Festivals

In mid-May, Valencia is the setting for a carnival called *Fallas*, a local word meaning "fire". Huge, papier-maché figures decorate the town's squares for a week, then are burnt in enormous fires. Alicante holds a smaller, similar festival called *Fogueras* on June 24. In late April, the citizens of Alcoy re-enact a historic battle for the Festival of Moors and Christians, which ends with the Moors being driven from the town.

In Caravaca, Murcia, men in magnificent costumes gather for the annual re-enactment of a battle between the Moors and Christians. Such ceremonies are also held in many other parts of the country.

Heavy with ornamentation, the 18th-century façade of Murcia's cathedral is one of Spain's outstanding examples of baroque architecture. The wealth of carvings represent scenes from paradise and the figures of the saints.

Andalucía

Picked out on its hilltop against a background of snow-capped peaks, Granada's Alhambra, or "Red Fort", glows in the evening sun. The exotic and splendid palace fortress remains Spain's finest example of Moorish artistry.

Andalucía is what most people imagine when they think of Spain: blazing sun, whitewashed villages and Moorish castles, the land of *Carmen* and of flamenco music performed by sloe-eyed gypsies. But this view, shared by the thousands of tourists who flock to the sun-drenched beaches of the Costa del Sol, is far too simplified. Andalucía hides many contrasts.

West of the Costa del Sol lies the Costa de la Luz, the Coast of Light, as unspoilt as its neighbour is developed; the Coto Doñana national park is one of Europe's richest nature reserves. Only a few hours from the golden beaches rise the icy ramparts of the Sierra Nevada. And while flamenco seems to typify the fiery Spanish character, Andalucía's Arabian architecture, its apricots and almonds, even the habit of outdoor cooking, make it more reminiscent of North Africa. The famed

Alhambra—the "Red Fort"—in Granada and the Mosque of Córdoba testify to the grandeur of the Moorish rule that endured here for over 700 years.

Andalucían cookery and life style reflect a climate that is itself more African than European. Western Europe's highest temperature, 45°C, was recorded in the Guadalquivir Valley. Local dishes match the weather; easy to prepare and light to eat, they range from fried fish to gazpacho, a cold vegetable soup based on tomatoes, garlic and bread which has become a classic of international summer cuisine.

In the hottest months, Andalucíans often go without a proper meal: as a local saying observes, "In Seville people don't eat meals, they nibble *tapas*." Bars offer these appetizers in such abundance that they fill both the evening and the stomach. There are Spanish olives, of which Andalucía is the home; tiny fish and prawns, fried and served in little bowls with a spicy sauce; different types of cold meats and sausages; crispy potato balls; and mushrooms and other vegetables served in a variety of marinades. Other local delicacies include hard, air-dried hams from Jabugo and Trevélez, and *huevos a la flamenca*, eggs lightly fried and garnished with vegetables from the fertile plains of Granada. As in the Levant, confectionery is based on almonds, pine-nuts, honey, cinnamon and eggs: *yemas*, or candied egg yolks, are particularly popular.

The glory of Andalucía, however, is sherry, a blend of wines fortified with spirits such as brandy. Sherry is the traditional accompaniment to *tapas*: the word *tapa* means literally a "lid" and originally referred to a little piece of bread, placed on top of the sherry glass to keep the flies off. Traditionally, between *tapas* you sip a dry light *fino* with a delicate almond taste. Sweeter sherries go better with dessert.

Sherry derives its name from the town of Jerez de la Frontera, and although many countries produce sherry-like wines, only that from Jerez is authentic. The finest and most famous sherry producers still have their headquarters in the town. In the massive *bodegas* or storehouses, large oak butts, or barrels, are stored in rows stacked up to five layers high while the sherry ferments to achieve its optimum flavour.

There are four basic types: *fino* is dry and pale; *amontillado* is darker in colour and a little sweeter; *oloroso*, which means "fragrant", is a deep amber and accompanies desserts; while cream sherry, thicker and syrupy, is the sweetest of all. The Spanish, however, prefer their sherry dry.

One of the prettiest of Andalucía's famed white towns, Vejer de la Frontera perches on a rocky crag above the Costa de la Luz. The town's quaint beauty belies its former role as a border stronghold during the occupation of Granada by the Moors.

Festivals

Andalucía is rich in festivals marking its distinctive character. Each September Jerez celebrates the grape harvest; in April or May, it stages a horse show. Córdoba hosts a flamenco festival in May, while Whitsun sees a gypsy pilgrimage to El Rocío. At the end of June, a music and dance festival takes place in Granada. Some of the most spectacular festivals, however, occur in Seville, which not only stages a *Feria*, or folklore festival in April, but is also the site of Spain's most elaborate celebration of Holy Week.

Little girls in traditional Andalucían costume celebrate the annual spring festival at Niebla, west of Seville.

The Balearic and Canary Islands

Spain's island groups—the Balearics in the Mediterranean and the Canaries in the Atlantic off North Africa—both suffered for many years from their popularity as holiday destinations. Concrete monstrosities threatened their picturesque coasts, while a tide of fast food swamped their respective cuisines. Yet the damage has now been largely halted: the islands have recaptured some of their original beauty, and local restaurants are returning more and more to traditional regional specialities.

Cooking on the island of Majorca, the largest of the Balearics—the others are Minorca, Ibiza and tiny Formentera—is dominated by pork, sausages, figs and almonds. The flavourings and seasoning of the more sophisticated dishes often reveal strong Moorish influences, as does the frequent combination of meat and fruit: turkey with almonds, for example, chicken served with pomegranates and pork or veal with figs, almonds and raisins.

As in those parts of the mainland that fell under Moorish sway, almonds are the basis of many sweetmeats, from almond milk to almond ice cream. Another delicacy comes from the old town of Palma, the regional capital, where many street corners house historic bakers' ovens called *forns*. In these are baked fresh *ensaimadas*, bulging snail-shaped spirals of sweet yeast dough, which range in size from a small breakfast version to enormous wagon wheels. Fresh fruit is provided by the citrus plantations of Sóller, on the island's northern coast.

The three smaller islands are less agricultural than Majorca, and their cooking is dominated by fish from the waters of the Mediterranean: mussels and other shellfish, for example, are often added to traditional fish soups. Minorca, however, also produces its own cheese, hard tangy *queso de Mahón*, which resembles Parmesan.

Good red and white wines come

Young women in traditional costume join in the annual Festival of the Brave Women, celebrated every May in Sóller on Majorca.

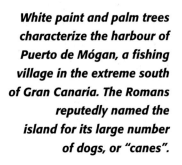

White paint and palm trees characterize the harbour of Puerto de Mógan, a fishing village in the extreme south of Gran Canaria. The Romans reputedly named the island for its large number of dogs, or "canes".

from the cellars of Binisalem and Felanitx on Majorca. There are also a number of interesting *digestifs*—liqueurs made from herbs, leaves, flowers or citrus fruits.

The Canary Islands are 10 times as close to Morocco as they are to Spain, and their landscapes have a North African character, with rain-starved cactus deserts on their southern sides and lush tropical plant cover.

The islands' cuisine shows not only Moorish influences, but also African and even South American. *Gofio*, a roasted maize meal which dates back to the Canaries' original inhabitants, the Guanches, is often served in place of bread. Another popular dish is a characteristic sauce called *mojo*, which is often used as a dip: mild *mojo verde* is made with lots of parsley, coriander and cumin, while a hot version, *mojo picón*, contains paprika, chili and garlic.

Canary Island desserts tend to be oriental in flavour and sickly-sweet, but the islands are major fruit growers and there is an especially plentiful supply of bananas, prickly pears and refreshing *nísperos*, or medlars.

The best Canary wine comes from the islands of Hierro and Lanzarote. The heavy sweet or dry Malmsey from Tenerife is drunk diluted, as a refresher or aperitif.

Festivals

Majorca has a number of major celebrations. In early May a re-enacted battle marks the Festival of the Brave Women, which commemorates a 15th-century episode when the women of Sóller saved their town from pirate attack. The island's capital, Palma, hosts an annual culinary fair each May where many delicious foods can be sampled. And in September, the Vilafranca de Bonany is home to a melon festival.

Past glories and present pleasures meet in the Canary Islands. Now relatively unimposing, Betancuría on Fuerteventura (top) was once the island's capital and royal city. At a seafront restaurant in Arrieta in the north of Lanzarote (above) diners enjoy fresh fish served with delicious sweet potatoes.

TAPAS

For most Spaniards, the working day ends with an *aperitivo*, enjoyed at home or, more often than not, at a local bar in the company of friends or colleagues. This uniquely Spanish way of sharpening the appetite traditionally consists of a glass of chilled *fino* or *manzanilla* sherry, accompanied by an array of little snacks known as *tapas*—the name derives from the original practice of using a piece of bread as a lid (*tapa*) to keep flies off the wine. A popular social pastime is to visit a number of bars throughout the evening, eating a selection of different *tapas* at each, in place of a full-blown dinner.

Tapas, which are also eaten before the midday meal, are endlessly varied. They range from such simple delights as salted almonds, stuffed olives, smoked *serrano* ham or Manchego cheese, to more substantial hot or cold specialities such as kidneys with sherry, fried or marinated anchovies, deep-fried squid rings and the famous *tortilla*, or potato omelette.

Such is the variety and versatility of these appetizers that they are also becoming increasingly popular outside Spain. Because they are easy to prepare in advance as well as delicious to eat, they are a simple and inexpensive way of entertaining, and offer something to suit every taste.

Albóndigas en salsa de tomate

Meat balls in tomato sauce

Needs a little time • Many regions

Serves 4 to 6

1 large onion
6 tbsp olive oil
5 cl dry (fino) sherry
750 g beef tomatoes
1 bay leaf
12.5 cl meat stock
300 g minced beef
300 g minced pork
2 garlic cloves
30 g flat-leaf parsley
2 eggs
3 tbsp fresh breadcrumbs
salt
freshly ground black pepper
hot paprika

Preparation time: 1 hour

2,800 kJ/670 calories per portion
(if serving 6)

1 Peel and finely chop the onion. Heat 2 tbsp olive oil in a saucepan and sauté the chopped onion over low heat until soft. Add the sherry.

2 Plunge the tomatoes briefly in boiling water; skin and halve them and remove the seeds. Finely chop the flesh and add it to the pan, together with the bay leaf. Pour in the stock and slowly return to the boil. Cover the pan and simmer for about 30 minutes.

3 While the sauce is cooking, put the minced beef and pork in a bowl. Peel the garlic, crush the flesh and add it to the meat. Wash the parsley, shake dry and chop finely; set aside half and add the remainder to the meat. Add the

eggs and the breadcrumbs. Mix thoroughly and season well with salt, pepper and paprika.

4 With wet hands, shape the mixture into walnut-sized balls. Heat the remaining oil in a large frying pan and fry the meat balls over medium heat until brown all over. Remove and drain.

5 Season the tomato sauce with plenty of salt, pepper and paprika. Place the cooked meat balls in the sauce and simmer over low heat for 10 minutes. Sprinkle with the remaining parsley and serve with crusty white bread.

Cebolletas al vinagre de jerez

Simple • Andalucía

Pearl onions in sherry vinegar

Serves 4 to 6

500 g pearl onions (or shallots)
6 tbsp olive oil
15 cl sherry vinegar
1 clove
1 dried chili pepper
1 sprig thyme
1 bay leaf
1 tsp black peppercorns
1 tsp salt
sugar

Preparation time: 1 hour
(plus about 1 hour cooling time)

750 kJ/180 calories per portion
(if serving 6)

1 Peel the onions but leave them whole. Heat the oil in a wide sauté pan and fry the onions over medium heat until golden.

2 Pour in the vinegar and ¼ litre water. Add the clove, chili pepper, thyme, bay leaf, peppercorns, salt and a little sugar.

3 Cover the pan and simmer over medium heat for about 30 minutes. Remove from the heat and leave to stand until completely cool.

Note: Pearl onions cooked in this way are also delicious served with grilled or stewed meat or game. The characteristic taste and spicy acidity of sherry vinegar adds a distinctive flavour to sauces, meat dishes, vegetables and salads. It is available from all good supermarkets and delicatessens.

Pimientos en adobo

Simple • La Rioja   **Marinated red peppers**   *Serves 4*

**4 large sweet red peppers
(about 1 kg)
4 garlic cloves
salt
freshly ground black pepper
hot paprika
20 cl virgin olive oil
1 tbsp sherry vinegar**

**Preparation time: 35 minutes
(plus at least 2 hours marinating
time)**

2,100 kJ/500 calories per portion

1 Light the grill or preheat the oven to 250°C (475°F or Mark 9). Wash the peppers, wipe dry and place under the grill—turning at intervals—or in the oven for 10 to 12 minutes, until the skins are scorched and blistered. Place in a covered bowl, or closed paper bag; the effect of the steam will make the peppers easier to peel. When they are cool enough to handle, peel them using a paring knife.

2 Meanwhile, peel the garlic cloves and cut them into thin slices.

3 Cut the sweet peppers in half, remove the seeds and ribs, and cut the flesh into strips about 2 cm wide.

Place the strips in a bowl and season with salt, pepper and paprika.

4 Scatter the sliced garlic over the peppers and pour over the oil and the vinegar, making sure that the peppers are well coated in the marinade. Cover, and refrigerate for at least 2 hours.

Variation: In the Basque country, skinned strips of sweet pepper are briefly fried in oil, then seasoned with a touch of chili, garlic, salt and pepper.

Note: Marinated sweet peppers are also a delicious accompaniment to grilled meat.

Riñones al jerez

Not difficult • Andalucía   **Kidneys in sherry**   *Serves 4 (or 2 as a main course)*

**1 calf's kidney (about 400 g)
milk for soaking
1 onion
1 garlic clove
2 tbsp virgin olive oil
20 cl dry (fino) sherry
1 small bay leaf
salt
freshly ground black pepper**

**Preparation time: 35 minutes
(plus 30 minutes soaking time)**

760 kJ/180 calories per portion

1 Cut the kidney in half lengthwise, peel off the surface membrane and cut out the fatty core. Rinse the kidney and place it in a bowl. Add enough milk to cover and leave to soak for at least 30 minutes.

2 Meanwhile, peel and finely chop the onion. Peel the garlic.

3 Remove the kidney from the milk, pat dry, then cut into medium-thin slices. Heat the oil in a frying pan and fry the slices, in batches if necessary, over high heat. Remove and set aside.

4 Add the chopped onion to the pan and sauté over medium heat until soft. Crush the garlic and add it to the pan. Add the sherry and the bay leaf, and simmer for about 3 minutes. Season the kidney slices with salt and pepper and return them, together with any juices, to the pan. Heat through for a further 3 minutes. Serve immediately, with fresh white bread.

Variation: Chicken livers can be substituted for the calf's kidney.

Croquetas de pollo

Chicken croquettes

Needs a little care • Many regions

Makes about 16 croquettes

*1 boned and skinned chicken breast
(about 150 g)*
1 tbsp virgin olive oil
1 garlic clove
salt
freshly ground white pepper
2 tbsp butter
3 to 4 tbsp flour
¼ litre milk
freshly ground nutmeg
5 tbsp fresh breadcrumbs
1 egg
oil for frying (see page 71)

*Preparation time: 50 minutes
(plus 30 minutes chilling time)*

1,000 kJ/240 calories per croquette

1 Heat the 1 tbsp olive oil in a frying pan and fry the chicken for about 10 minutes over medium heat, until lightly browned. Meanwhile, peel and crush the garlic, sprinkle over the chicken, and season with salt and pepper. Remove the chicken from the pan and set it aside to cool.

2 Melt the butter over low heat in a saucepan. Add the 2 tbsp flour and, stirring, cook for about 2 minutes. Slowly pour in the milk, blending with a whisk to prevent lumps from forming. Whisking continuously, cook for a further 6 to 8 minutes, until the sauce thickens. Remove from the heat.

3 Using a food processor, mince the chicken very finely, then stir it into the white sauce. Season generously with

salt, pepper and nutmeg. Refrigerate for about 30 minutes.

4 With floured hands, shape the mixture into small croquettes. Put the remaining flour and the breadcrumbs on separate plates. Whisk the egg on a third plate. Dip each croquette first in the flour, then in the beaten egg and finally in the breadcrumbs, rolling it so that it is completely coated.

5 Fill a deep-sided frying pan with a generous amount of oil and fry the croquettes for 3 to 4 minutes, until golden. Remove from the pan and drain on kitchen paper. Serve hot or cold.

Variation: The croquettes can also be made with ham, salt cod or veal.

Ensalada de zanahoria

Carrot salad

Not difficult • Andalucía

Serves 4 to 6

500 g carrots
2 garlic cloves
3 tbsp white wine vinegar
4 tbsp virgin olive oil
1 tsp ground cumin
½ tsp mild paprika
*1 to 2 tsp fresh chopped oregano
leaves, or ½ tsp dried oregano*
salt
freshly ground black pepper

*Preparation time: 35 minutes
(plus 4 to 12 hours marinating time)*

*360 kJ/86 calories per portion
(if serving 6)*

1 Wash and peel the carrots. Put them in a saucepan, add just enough water to cover the carrots and bring to the boil. Reduce the heat to medium, cover the pan and cook for 10 to 15 minutes, or until tender.

2 Meanwhile, peel and finely chop the garlic and mix it with the vinegar, olive oil, cumin, paprika, oregano, salt and pepper.

3 Drain the carrots and cut them into 5 mm-thick slices. Stir the slices into the marinade and leave to marinate for at least 4 hours, preferably overnight.

Note: Carrot salad goes well with meat or poultry *tapas* and is also good served as a side dish with grills. Cumin, a spice native to the Mediterranean region, was introduced to Spain by the Moors. It is also widely cultivated in Asia and an ingredient in many curries and meat dishes. Similar in appearance to caraway seeds, it is available either whole or ground but should be used sparingly, as it has a pungent aroma and a strong, hot flavour.

Pipirrana

Simple • Málaga **Summer salad**

1 small sweet red pepper
1 small sweet green pepper
1 small cucumber
1 small Spanish onion
2 beef tomatoes (about 400 g)
4 tbsp red wine vinegar
salt
freshly ground black pepper
5 tbsp virgin olive oil
3 or 4 garlic cloves

Preparation time: 30 minutes
(plus 1 hour marinating time)

470 kJ/110 calories per portion
(if serving 6)

1 Wash the peppers; cut them in half lengthwise and remove the stalk, seeds and ribs. Peel the cucumber, cut it in half lengthwise and scrape out the seeds with a spoon. Peel the onion. Finely dice all three vegetables and place in a bowl.

2 Plunge the tomatoes briefly in boiling water, skin, halve and remove the seeds. Dice the flesh and add it to the other vegetables.

3 Mix the vinegar with the salt, pepper and olive oil. Peel the garlic cloves, crush them and stir into the vinaigrette.

Pour the dressing over the vegetables and stir in thoroughly. Leave to marinate in the refrigerator for about 1 hour. Serve with white bread.

Variation: Salpicón de mariscos
(Shellfish salad)
Prepare half the quantity of the salad above, then toss in cooked shellfish, such as scampi, mussels or scallops.

Note: *Pipirrana* is also an ideal accompaniment to meat or poultry.

Pinchos morunos

Not difficult • Córdoba   **Moorish-style kebabs**   *Serves 4 (or 2 as a main course)*

600 g pork fillet
1 tsp ground cumin
2 tbsp mild paprika
5 tbsp olive oil
salt
freshly ground black pepper
cayenne pepper
4 cocktail tomatoes

Preparation time: 30 minutes
(plus 1 hour marinating time)

1,600 kJ/380 calories per portion

1 Cut the pork fillet into little cubes about 2 cm square.

2 In a large bowl, mix the cumin, paprika, olive oil, some salt and pepper and a little cayenne pepper. Add the meat cubes to the marinade, mix well and refrigerate for about 1 hour.

3 Preheat the grill. Thread the cubes of meat tightly onto small wooden skewers (about 20) and grill them for 10 to 12 minutes, turning frequently and basting with the marinade, until well browned. (Alternatively, they can be fried over medium heat.) Garnish with the cocktail tomatoes cut in half, and serve with white bread.

Variation: If serving this dish as a main course, cut the meat into larger cubes and increase the cooking time slightly. Accompany it with mashed potatoes and a green vegetable or a mixed salad.

Note: These highly spiced kebabs were originally made only with lamb. Such dishes date back to the Moorish occupation of Spain, when many new foods and seasonings were introduced, among them spices such as cumin.

Tortilla de gambas

Prawn omelette

Quick and easy · Many regions

Serves 4

**200 g cooked, shelled deep sea
prawns
juice of ½ lemon
3 tbsp olive oil
4 eggs
salt
freshly ground black pepper**

Preparation time: 20 minutes

1,100 kJ/260 calories per portion

1 Place the prawns in a bowl and sprinkle them with the lemon juice.

2 Heat the olive oil in a frying pan about 20 cm in diameter, and briefly toss the prawns in the oil.

3 Whisk the eggs thoroughly with a little salt and pepper. Pour the beaten eggs over the prawns in the pan and cook over low heat for about 5 minutes, until the omelette begins to set.

4 Remove the pan from the heat. Invert a plate over the pan and flip the omelette onto it. Carefully slide the omelette back into the pan and cook the second side for a further 5 minutes.

5 Cut the omelette into wedges or bite-sized cubes and serve, hot or cold, with fresh white bread.

Variations: Tortillas come with an endless variety of fillings and many can be served as *tapas*. For example, instead of the prawns, finely dice 3 medium-sized green peppers, 1 onion and 1 skinned, deseeded beef tomato and sauté them in the oil until soft; then pour on the beaten egg and proceed as above. Or, for a spinach tortilla, mix 400 g sautéed spinach leaves with a little garlic and 1 tbsp toasted pine-nuts.

Ensaladilla rusa

Russian salad

Not difficult · Many regions

Serves 4 to 6

**750 g waxy potatoes
200 g French beans
salt
150 g carrots
150 g freshly shelled, or frozen,
peas
freshly ground black pepper
4 tbsp sherry vinegar
3 egg yolks (see Note)
1 tbsp lemon juice
¼ litre olive oil**

**Preparation time: 45 minutes
(plus 30 minutes chilling time)**

**2,200 kJ/520 calories per portion
(if serving 6)**

1 Wash the potatoes. Place in a pan, cover with water and bring to the boil. Cook until tender but still firm.

2 Meanwhile, trim and wash the green beans. Bring a pan of salted water to the boil, add the beans and cook for about 10 minutes. Peel and finely dice the carrots, put them, together with the fresh peas, in another pan of boiling salted water and cook for about 5 minutes—if using frozen peas, add 1 to 2 minutes before end of cooking time.

3 Drain all three vegetables, rinse in cold water, drain again thoroughly, and place in a mixing bowl.

4 Peel the potatoes and dice them into 1 cm cubes. Add to the rest of the vegetables. Season the mixture with salt and pepper and sprinkle with the sherry vinegar.

5 In another bowl, combine the egg yolks with the lemon juice, salt and pepper. Whisking vigorously, add the olive oil very gradually, to make a creamy mayonnaise. Mix the dressing into the vegetables and refrigerate for about 30 minutes.

Note: Use only very fresh eggs from a source you trust—uncooked eggs may carry the salmonella bacteria that causes food poisoning.

Gambas al ajillo

Garlic prawns

500 g fresh raw prawns
2 fresh, or dried, red chili peppers
(see Glossary)
6 or 8 garlic cloves
20 cl olive oil
salt
freshly ground black pepper

Preparation time: 20 minutes

2,400 kJ/570 calories per portion

1 Shell the prawns, removing the heads and dark, vein-like intestines. Rinse in cold water and pat dry.

2 Wash the chilis and halve them lengthwise. Remove the seeds and cut into thin rings. (If using dried chilies, crush them in a mortar.) Peel the garlic and quarter lengthwise.

3 Heat the olive oil in a frying pan. Add the chilies, garlic and prawns. Lightly season with salt and pepper and cook over high heat for 2 to 3 minutes.

4 Serve immediately in small dishes, accompanied by fresh white bread.

Note: Garlic prawns are one of the most popular *tapas*; they are often served in the same small pans or earthenware dishes in which they were cooked. Freshly cooked or frozen prawns can be used instead of raw ones. If using cooked prawns, heat them only very briefly; otherwise they will be tough. A good, mild-tasting olive oil is best for this dish.

Garlic

The bulbs of this aromatic and pungent plant, familiar since ancient times, are a classic ingredient of many national cuisines, notably those of the Mediterranean. One of the largest producers of garlic is Spain, where it is used in generous amounts in fish, meat and poultry dishes, as well as in sausages, soups and sauces.

Long celebrated for its nutritive and medicinal properties, research indicates that garlic promotes the circulation of blood to the brain.

There are two basic types of garlic available all year round: *ajo blanco*,

the universal white garlic, and the more expensive *ajo morado* with a reddish-violet skin, which is exported in large quantities. The fresher the garlic, the better the flavour and nutritive value will be. Always choose fresh, plump

bulbs—they should be rock hard—and avoid those showing green shoots, as these can impart a bitter taste to food. Stored in a cool dry place, exposed to the air, garlic should keep for several months.

Pechuga de pollo en jerez

Quick and easy • Andalucía **Chicken in sherry** *Serves 4*

600 g boned and skinned chicken breast
salt
flour for coating
2 tbsp olive oil
freshly ground black pepper
¼ litre dry (fino) sherry
12.5 cl chicken stock
2 garlic cloves
1 sprig thyme
1 small jar (about 60 g) olives stuffed with sweet red pepper

Preparation time: 40 minutes

1,100 kJ/260 calories per portion

1 Cut the chicken breast into 3 cm-long pieces, season with salt, and roll them in flour to coat.

2 Heat the olive oil in a large frying pan and briefly fry the chicken pieces over high heat until browned. Season with salt and pepper, remove from the pan and set aside.

3 Pour off the remaining oil and return the pan to the heat. Add the sherry, then stir in the chicken stock. Peel the garlic cloves, crush them and add to the pan. Break the sprig of thyme into small pieces and add to the sauce. Cook the sauce, uncovered, until reduced to about one third of its original volume.

4 Return the chicken pieces to the pan and simmer over low heat for about 10 minutes. Meanwhile, slice the stuffed olives, add them to the pan and heat through. Serve immediately, with crusty white bread.

Champiñones rellenos

Stuffed mushrooms

Not difficult • Extremadura

Serves 4 to 6

16 to 20 large button mushrooms
1 small onion
2 tbsp olive oil
300 g chorizos (see page 56)
1 garlic clove
30 g flat-leaf parsley
salt
freshly ground black pepper
1 tsp mild paprika
tomatoes for garnish (optional)

Preparation time: 55 minutes

880 kJ/210 calories per portion (if serving 6)

1 Trim the mushrooms, rinse briefly or wipe with a cloth. Pull off the stalks and chop finely. Set the caps aside.

2 Preheat the oven to 220°C (425°F or Mark 7). Peel and finely chop the onion. Heat half the olive oil in a frying pan and sauté the onion over medium heat. Add the chopped mushroom stalks and continue to cook until most of the liquid has evaporated.

3 Skin the chorizos, or squeeze the sausage meat straight from the skin into the pan. Stir it into the onion and mushroom mixture. Peel the garlic, crush the flesh and add it to the pan. Fry over low heat for about 8 minutes.

4 Meanwhile, wash the parsley, shake dry and chop finely. Season the sausage mixture with salt, pepper and the paprika. Remove the pan from the heat and leave to cool a little, then stir in the chopped parsley.

5 Stuff each mushroom cap with a little of the sausage mixture. Grease a baking dish with the remaining oil and arrange the stuffed mushrooms side by side in the dish. Bake in the centre of the oven for 10 to 12 minutes, until the mushrooms begin to brown. Serve with white bread and, if you like, tomatoes cut into segments.

Boquerones en vinagre

Marinated anchovies

600 g fresh anchovies (or sprats or smelts)
12.5 cl sherry vinegar
10 garlic cloves
30 g flat-leaf parsley
salt
freshly ground black pepper
¼ litre virgin olive oil

Preparation time: 25 minutes
(plus 2½ hours marinating time)

4,200 kJ/1,000 calories per portion

1 To gut the fish, run your index finger or a knife along the belly. Gently pull the head free, then open the fish out flat and peel the head and backbone away from the flesh (*above*), pinching it loose at the tail. Wash thoroughly under cold running water and pat dry.

2 Press each fish flat into a "butterfly" shape and lay them in a shallow baking dish. Mix the sherry vinegar with ¼ litre water and pour it over the fish (*above*). Leave to marinate for 1 to 1½ hours, until the flesh has whitened.

3 Meanwhile, peel and finely chop the garlic cloves—do not use a garlic crusher. Wash the parsley, shake dry and chop coarsely.

4 Pour off the marinade and briefly rinse the fish under cold running water. Return them to the baking dish, season with salt and pepper, and sprinkle with the chopped garlic and parsley (*above*). Finally, pour the oil over the anchovies and leave them to marinate for a further hour, or until ready to use. Serve with crusty white bread.

Drink: Beer goes well with this dish.

Variation:
Deep-fried anchovies
Fried anchovies are also popular served as *tapas*. Leave the fish whole, season with salt and pepper, and coat with flour. Deep fry in olive oil until golden-brown and crisp. Serve hot, with lemon wedges.

Note: Marinated anchovies with jacket potatoes make a delicious informal supper. Fresh anchovies are imported by good fishmongers but, if unavailable, sprats or smelts are good alternatives.

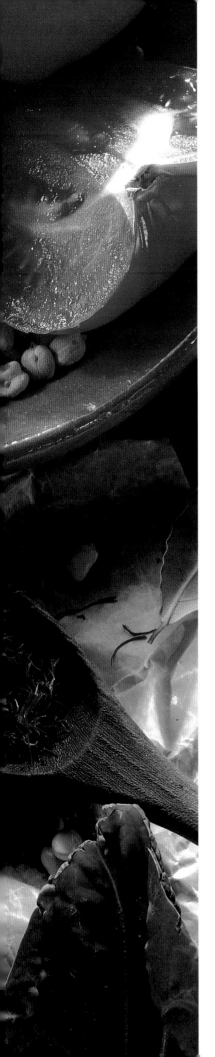

SOUPS AND STEWS

S panish soups and stews range from light first courses to complete one-pot meals. The latter are by far the more common: soups are traditionally hearty and substantial, reflecting their origins as cheap but filling dishes for the poor. Pulses are the foundation of many delicious stews throughout Spain, and are a traditional part of meatless lenten meals. But rich stews also depend on meat or fish, and every region has its own specialities which use the bounty of the surrounding land or sea. So distinctive are some of these recipes that they are almost bywords for local pride and tradition: the *cocidos* of Castile and Madrid, for example, made with boiled meats, sausages and chick-peas, or the bean and sausage *fabada* of Asturias. The coastal regions offer marvellous fish and seafood stews such as the renowned *zarzuela* from Catalonia (*see page 82*).

Among the lighter soups is the garlic soup, *sopa de ajo*, which originally consisted only of water, bread and garlic, but now appears in a range of more sophisticated forms. In the baking-hot climate of Andalucía, ice-cold gazpacho makes a refreshing first course. The standard version is tomato-based and red, but regional variations include a white type from Extremadura and a creamy, almond version from Málaga called *ajo blanco*.

Sopa de almendras

Fairly easy • Andalucía

Almond and saffron soup

Serves 4

200 g almonds
5 garlic cloves
8 slices day-old white bread
30 g flat-leaf parsley
5 tbsp olive oil
salt
freshly ground black pepper
cumin
200 mg saffron
¾ litre meat stock

Preparation time: 50 minutes

2,200 kJ/520 calories per portion

1 Drop the almonds into boiling water and leave for 1 to 2 minutes, until the skins begin to loosen, then drain. Wrap in a towel and rub vigorously to remove the skins. Peel the garlic. Cut the bread into small dice. Wash and dry the parsley, remove the stalks and reserve the leaves.

2 Heat the oil in a frying pan and fry the bread, tossing frequently, until crisp and golden. Remove from the pan with a slotted spoon and reserve.

3 Add the almonds and garlic to the pan and cook over medium heat until they are golden. Add half the parsley and fry for about 3 minutes more. Purée in a food processor or vegetable mill, until smooth.

4 Transfer the purée to a heavy pan and season with salt, pepper, a little cumin and the saffron. Stir in the stock and slowly bring to the boil. Reduce the heat to low, cover the pan and simmer for about 20 minutes.

5 Meanwhile, finely chop the rest of the parsley. When the soup is cooked, stir in half the fried bread and check the seasoning, as bread absorbs flavour. Serve hot, garnished with chopped parsley and the rest of the bread.

Saffron

The dried, orange-red stigmas of the saffron crocus have long been valued for their pungent flavour and exotic aroma, and for the brilliant yellow hue they give to food. It was used by both Greeks and Romans, but it was the Arabs who introduced the spice to the Iberian peninsula, where it still features in many dishes, particularly rice dishes.

Spain, where the purple flowers flourish especially in the dry soil of Castile-La Mancha, produces two-thirds of the world's saffron supply —hence the spice's other name, "Castillian Gold". Until recently, indeed, saffron was dearer than gold and it is still the world's most expensive spice, retailing at about £5,000 per kilogram. The cost of saffron reflects the intensive labour required to produce it. Only the three stigmas from each flower are used, and it requires about 170 blooms to produce a single gram of spice. The plants flower over-night around mid-October, covering the fields with a carpet of purple; to preserve their flavour, they are picked by hand the same day in hours of back-breaking toil. The stigmas are then plucked from the flowers, spread on trays and dried over charcoal fires.

Saffron is available in threads— the dried stigmas—or ground into powder; the threads generally have more flavour than the powder. It is sold in sachets, glass jars or small tins. Because of its strong flavour, it is always used sparingly.

Sopa de ajo

Not difficult · Castile   **Garlic soup**   *Serves 4*

300 g day-old white bread
1 garlic head
4 tbsp olive oil
1 tsp mild paprika
salt
freshly ground black pepper
1 litre meat stock
4 eggs

Preparation time: 1 hour

2,000 kJ/480 calories per portion

1 Cut the bread into small dice. Break the garlic into cloves and peel them.

2 In a frying pan, heat the olive oil and fry the bread over medium heat, tossing frequently, until golden-brown. Crush the garlic cloves and add to the pan. Sprinkle with the paprika and season with salt and pepper. Pour in the stock, bring to the boil, then reduce the heat to low, cover and simmer for about 20 minutes. Meanwhile, preheat the oven to 200°C (400°F or Mark 6).

3 Pour the soup into four individual ovenproof earthenware bowls. One at a time, break the eggs carefully into a ladle or cup and gently slide one into each bowl of soup.

4 Place the bowls in the centre of the oven and bake for about 10 minutes, until the eggs set. Serve immediately.

Note: Every region has its own version of garlic soup. Sometimes it is made with water, sometimes with stock, in some areas it might also contain, for example, tomatoes and peppers. One version in Cadiz—served sprinkled with grated cheese—is known locally as *Sopa de gato,* or cat soup.

Cazuela de lentejas

Fairly easy · Catalonia   **Lentil casserole**   *Serves 4 to 6*

1 garlic head
1 large onion
2 cloves
1 sweet green pepper
1 ripe beef tomato
3 tbsp olive oil
1 tsp mild paprika
hot paprika
cumin
500 g lentils
1 bay leaf
2 floury potatoes (about 450 g)
500 g chorizos (see page 56)
salt
freshly ground black pepper

Preparation time: 1½ hours

3,700 kJ/880 calories per portion (if serving 6)

1 Preheat the oven to 180°C (350°F or Mark 4). Place the garlic head on a rack or griddle and bake in the oven for about 15 minutes. Remove and leave to cool.

2 Meanwhile, peel the onion and spike it with the cloves. Wash the green pepper and cut it in half. Remove the stalk, ribs and seeds, and cut the flesh into strips. Plunge the tomato briefly into boiling water. Skin, halve and deseed, and coarsely chop the flesh. Carefully peel the baked garlic cloves and crush into a pulp.

3 Heat the oil in a large casserole or heavy saucepan. Briefly sauté the tomato and green pepper, then stir in the mild paprika, a pinch of hot paprika and a little cumin. Add the lentils, onion, bay leaf and ¾ litre water. Stir in the crushed garlic. Bring to the boil, cover the pan and simmer over low heat for about 45 minutes, until the lentils are tender.

4 Meanwhile, peel and wash the potatoes. Dice them finely and stir into the pan after about 30 minutes of cooking. Add the chorizos for the last 5 minutes. Before serving, remove and discard the onion and bay leaf and season the casserole with salt and freshly ground pepper. Serve hot with crusty white bread.

Wine: A strong red wine from Navarre or Rioja is especially good with this dish.

Purrusalda

Salt cod stew

Serves 4

500 g dried salt cod
750 g leeks
2 garlic cloves
500 g floury potatoes
5 tbsp olive oil
1 bay leaf
salt
freshly ground black pepper
1 tsp mild paprika

Preparation time: 1¼ hours
(plus at least 24 hours soaking
time)

2,800 kJ/670 calories per portion

1 Soak the salt cod in cold water for at least 24 hours, changing the water three or four times. The fish is ready for cooking when it has roughly doubled in size.

2 Remove the cod from the water, rinse and reserve. Trim and wash the leeks, and cut into thin rings. Peel the garlic cloves and halve lengthwise. Peel and wash the potatoes and cut into 5 mm slices.

3 Heat the olive oil in a fireproof casserole or heavy saucepan. Add the garlic and fry over medium heat, stirring constantly, until golden. Remove from the pan with a slotted spoon and set aside. Add the leeks to the remaining oil and sauté until soft.

4 Stir in the potatoes, add the bay leaf and season with a little salt and plenty of pepper. Add ¾ litre water, bring to the boil, cover and simmer over low heat for about 30 minutes.

5 Meanwhile, crush the fried garlic with a pestle and mortar, or mash with a fork. Mix with the paprika and stir into the simmering vegetables.

6 Cut the fish into bite-sized pieces and add to the saucepan. Cook for about another 5 minutes, until the fish is cooked and flakes easily. Serve with crusty white bread.

Note: Salt cod is available from good fishmongers and some delicatessens.

Caldo de pescado

Fish soup

Serves 4

2 large onions
250 g ripe beef tomatoes
800 g sweet red peppers
3 tbsp olive oil
3 tsp mild paprika
3 large garlic cloves
salt
1 tsp coarsely crushed black pepper
1 tsp cumin
600 g firm-fleshed, white fish fillets
(for example, cod, pollack or hake)
2 tbsp lemon juice

Preparation time: 50 minutes

1,000 kJ/240 calories per portion

1 Peel and finely chop the onions. Plunge the tomatoes briefly into boiling water. Skin, halve and deseed them, and coarsely chop the flesh. Wash the sweet red peppers and cut them in half. Remove the stalks, ribs and seeds and cut the flesh into small dice.

2 In a large saucepan or fireproof casserole, heat the olive oil and sauté the onions over low heat until transparent. Add the tomatoes and the paprika, and stir in thoroughly. Cook over low heat for a further 5 minutes.

3 Peel the garlic and crush directly into the pan. Season with a little salt, half the pepper and the cumin.

4 Stir a third of the diced red peppers into the pan. Add ¾ litre water, bring to the boil, reduce the heat to low and simmer for about 20 minutes.

5 Meanwhile, rinse the fish under cold water, cut into bite-sized pieces, and sprinkle with the lemon juice. Season with salt and the remaining pepper.

6 Purée the soup in a food processor or vegetable mill and return to the pan. Add the fish and remaining peppers to the puréed soup and bring to the boil. Cover the pan and simmer for about 5 minutes. Serve with crusty bread.

Callos a la gallega

Takes a little time • Galicia　　**Stewed tripe with chorizo**　　　　　　　*Serves 6 to 8*

300 g dried chick-peas
750 g cooked tripe
2 tbsp vinegar
2 onions
6 garlic cloves
750 g ripe beef tomatoes
150 g serrano ham (or, if
unavailable, prosciutto)
4 tbsp olive oil
2 tsp fresh, or 1 tsp dried, thyme
salt • freshly ground black pepper
1 small, dried chili pepper (see
Glossary)
1 bay leaf
¾ litre meat stock
300 g chorizos (see below)
30 g flat-leaf parsley

Preparation time: 2¾ hours
(plus soaking time)

1,800 kJ/430 calories per portion
(if serving 8)

1 Soak the chick-peas overnight in cold water.

2 The next day, cover the tripe with cold water, add the vinegar and soak for about 30 minutes.

3 Meanwhile, peel and finely chop the onions and garlic. Plunge the tomatoes into boiling water, skin and deseed them and coarsely chop the flesh. Finely dice the ham.

4 In a large saucepan, heat the olive oil and sauté the onions, garlic and ham over low heat until the onions are transparent. Meanwhile, drain the tripe and cut it into thin strips and add to the pan.

5 Stir in the tomatoes, and season with the thyme and some salt and pepper. Crush the chili pepper slightly —for example, with the back of a spoon—and add to the pan with the bay leaf. Drain the chick-peas and stir into the pan. Add the stock, bring to the boil, cover and simmer over low heat for about 2 hours.

6 Slice the chorizos and add to the saucepan about 15 minutes before the end of the cooking time. Meanwhile, wash the parsley, shake dry, remove the stalks and finely chop the leaves. Remove the bay leaf from the stew and check the seasoning. Sprinkle with the chopped parsley and serve with crusty white bread.

Chorizo

Chorizo, a red paprika sausage, is one of the most common and distinctive ingredients of Spanish cooking: it can be sliced and eaten cold as an appetizer, or served grilled, or added to substantial and warming stews such as *Fabada asturiana* (*page 61*).

Each region has its own local version, with variations on the basic ingredients of salt pork and pork fillet, heavily scented with garlic and paprika. In León and Galicia, for example, chorizo is lightly smoked; in Pamplona in Navarre it contains beef, as well as a generous quantity of paprika, a pinch of sugar, but little garlic; in Salamanca, regarded by connoisseurs as Spain's chorizo capital, sherry adds extra richness to the sausage mixture. There is even a very garlicky variation that contains no paprika, called *chorizo blanco*.

Whatever the variety, chorizo is available smoked or air-dried. In Britain, it can be found in Spanish grocers, delicatessens and well-stocked supermarkets.

Ajo blanco con uvas

Not difficult • Málaga **Chilled grape and almond soup** *Serves 4*

3 slices white bread (about 80 g)
120 g almonds
3 garlic cloves
4 tbsp olive oil
1 tbsp white wine vinegar
salt
freshly ground white pepper
150 g white muscatel grapes

Preparation time: 20 minutes
(plus 1 hour chilling time)

1,500 kJ/360 calories per portion

1 Cut the crusts off the bread and discard. Soak the bread in cold water for about 10 minutes. Meanwhile, blanch the almonds (*page 50, Step 1*) and peel the garlic.

2 Squeeze as much moisture as possible from the bread, and purée with the garlic and almonds in a food processor or vegetable mill.

3 Place the purée in a large bowl and stir in the olive oil and ¾ litre water.

Add the white wine vinegar and season with plenty of salt and pepper. Cover the bowl and place in the refrigerator to chill for at least 1 hour.

4 Meanwhile, peel and halve the grapes, and remove the seeds.

5 Before serving, stir the soup thoroughly and check for seasoning. Serve in individual bowls, sprinkled with the grapes.

Gazpacho

Fairly easy • Andalucía **Cold vegetable soup** *Serves 4*

200 g white bread
10 cl olive oil
4 garlic cloves
cumin
750 g ripe beef tomatoes
1 cucumber
1 sweet green pepper
salt
2 tbsp red wine vinegar

Preparation time: 40 minutes
(plus at least 1 hour chilling time)

1,800 kJ/430 calories per portion

1 Reserve 50 g of the bread. Tear the rest into pieces, place in a bowl and sprinkle with the olive oil. Peel and crush the garlic and add to the bread. Sprinkle with a little cumin, stir thoroughly and leave to stand for about 30 minutes.

2 Meanwhile, plunge the tomatoes briefly into boiling water, skin, halve and deseed. Finely dice half of one tomato, place in a small bowl and reserve. Coarsely chop the rest and place in a food processor.

3 Peel the cucumber; finely dice about one third, place in a small bowl and reserve. Coarsely chop the rest and add to the tomatoes in the food processor.

4 Wash the green pepper and cut in half. Remove the stalk, ribs and seeds; finely dice about one third of the flesh, place in a small bowl and reserve.

Coarsely chop the remainder, and place in the food processor with the tomatoes and cucumber. Add the soaked bread and garlic, and purée the mixture until it is smooth.

5 Rub the purée through a fine sieve into a large bowl. If you prefer a soup with a thinner consistency, add ¼ litre water. Season with salt and stir in the wine vinegar. Place in the refrigerator, together with the small bowls of diced vegetables, and chill for at least 1 hour.

6 Cut the reserved bread into small dice and place in a serving bowl. Check the gazpacho for seasoning and serve accompanied by the bread and vegetable garnishes.

Note: On very hot days, ice cubes are often added to gazpacho. A food mill can be used instead of the food processor.

Potaje de garbanzos

Not difficult • Catalonia   **Chick-pea and spinach stew**   *Serves 4*

500 g dried chick-peas
2 onions
1 carrot
2 tbsp olive oil
1 bay leaf
salt
1 litre meat stock
4 garlic cloves
2 beef tomatoes (about 500 g)
300 g leaf spinach
freshly ground black pepper
3 eggs

Preparation time: 1¾ hours
(plus 12 hours soaking time)

2,600 kJ/620 calories per portion

1 Soak the chick-peas overnight in plenty of cold water.

2 Peel and finely chop the onions. Peel and slice the carrot. Heat the olive oil in a large saucepan and sauté the onions and carrot over low heat until the onions are transparent.

3 Drain the chick-peas and add to the pan together with the bay leaf. Season with salt, pour in the stock and slowly bring to the boil. Peel and halve the garlic cloves and stir into the chick-peas. Cover, and cook over medium-low heat for about 50 minutes. Remove and discard the bay leaf.

4 Meanwhile, plunge the tomatoes briefly into boiling water; skin, halve and deseed them, and coarsely chop the flesh. Wash, trim and coarsely chop the spinach. Stir the tomatoes and spinach into the chick-peas. Season with plenty of salt and pepper and cook for a further 20 minutes.

5 Meanwhile, in another saucepan, boil the eggs until hard boiled, about 10 minutes. Plunge into cold water to arrest cooking, shell, finely chop and place in a serving bowl. Check the stew for seasoning, as chick-peas absorb a lot of the flavour. Serve in individual dishes, sprinkled with chopped egg and accompanied by crusty white bread.

Fabada asturiana

Bean and sausage stew

**500 g large, dried white beans
(cannellini or haricot beans)
2 onions
4 garlic cloves
150 g rindless, streaky bacon
150 g serrano ham (or, if
unavailable, prosciutto)
2 tbsp olive oil
3 tbsp tomato purée
1 tbsp mild paprika • 1 bay leaf
salt • freshly ground black pepper
400 mg saffron
2 chorizos (about 300 g)
2 morcillas (about 300 g)**

**Preparation time: 2½ hours
(plus 12 hours soaking time)**

5,100 kJ/1,200 calories per portion

1 Soak the white beans overnight in plenty of water.

2 Peel and finely chop the onions and garlic. Finely chop the bacon and ham. Heat the olive oil in a large saucepan or fireproof casserole and sauté the onions and garlic until the onions are transparent. Stir in the tomato purée and paprika.

3 Drain the beans and add to the pan. Add the bacon, ham and bay leaf, and season with a little salt and pepper. Do not oversalt: the ham and sausages are both very salty. Add 1.5 litres water, bring to the boil, then reduce the heat to low, cover, and simmer for about 1½ hours. From time to time, skim off any scum that forms on the surface.

4 Season with a little more pepper and the saffron. Add the chorizos and the *morcillas* and cook for a further 30 minutes. Check the seasoning and adjust if necessary. Remove and discard the bay leaf. Serve with crusty white bread.

Wine: Valdeorras, a light, Asturian red wine, is a good choice with this dish.

Note: *Fabada asturiana*, the best-known of Spain's substantial bean stews, is just right for the cold winter evenings of the northwest. It can be prepared in advance and reheated. It can also be made with ingredients such as pig's ears, tails and trotters. *Morcilla* is a Spanish black pudding; if unavailable, omit or substitute a mild smoked sausage.

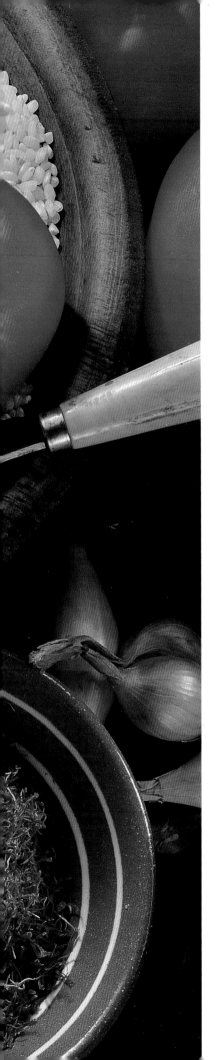

RICE, EGGS AND VEGETABLES

S panish cuisine is characterized by its inventive use of the most humble of ingredients such as rice, vegetables and eggs, all of which are in plentiful supply. In the vast marshland fields of Valencia grows the distinctive round-grain, starchy rice that lends itself to countless rice dishes. These vary from region to region and may include fish or seafood, meat, vegetables, poultry or, as in the case of paella, a mixture of all of them. This gloriously colourful medley of saffron rice, mixed seafood and vegetables—its name derives from the large pan in which it is traditionally cooked—is one of Spain's most celebrated creations.

Among the great delights of Spain are its busy vegetable markets, where the produce from many regions is displayed. Potatoes are a staple served with most main courses; however, fresh, unadorned vegetables are not generally a prominent feature of the country's cuisine. Instead, the Spanish prefer to stew or fry their vegetables, or combine them with other ingredients to make such dishes as *Huevos a la flamenca*—originally a gypsy dish— a delicious combination of mixed vegetables, ham and eggs.

Eggs also combine with potatoes to make another widespread and much-loved classic: *Tortilla de patatas*, or potato omelette. This simple and hearty dish has become a particular favourite, suitable for any occasion from a simple picnic or supper to a party.

Paella

Chicken and seafood rice

More complex • Valencia

Serves 6

2 sweet red peppers (about 300 g)
600 g beef tomatoes
1 large onion
5 garlic cloves
1 oven-ready chicken (about 1.2 kg)
250 g pork loin
400 g clams
6 raw deep-sea prawns
8 tbsp olive oil
salt
freshly ground black pepper
300 g freshly shelled, or frozen, peas
200 mg powdered saffron
1 tsp mild paprika
1 bay leaf
1.25 litres meat stock
500 g Spanish round-grain rice or Italian arborio rice
1 lemon

Preparation time: 2¼ hours

3,800 kJ/900 calories per portion

1 Light the grill or preheat the oven to 250°C (475°F or Mark 9). Wash the peppers, wipe dry, and remove the skins (*page 34, top recipe, Step 1*). Halve the skinned peppers, remove the seeds and ribs and cut into narrow strips. Reduce the oven temperature to 180°C (350°F or Mark 4),

2 Plunge the tomatoes briefly in boiling water, skin, halve and deseed. Coarsely chop the flesh. Peel and finely chop the onion and the garlic.

3 Divide the chicken into 12 pieces. Dice the pork. Scrub the clams under cold running water, removing the beards; discard any that remain open. Rinse the prawns.

4 Heat the olive oil in a paella or roasting pan (*see opposite page, Note*).

Fry the chicken pieces over high heat until brown all over, remove from the pan, season with salt and pepper and keep warm. Repeat with the diced pork. Add the clams to the pan and fry until they open; remove from the pan, discarding any that remain closed and keep warm. Finally, fry the prawns until they turn red, remove and keep warm.

5 In the remaining fat, sauté the chopped onion and garlic over medium heat until transparent. Add the tomatoes and the peas and sauté for about 5 minutes. Stir in the saffron and the paprika, then season generously with salt and pepper. Add the bay leaf.

6 In a saucepan, bring the meat stock to the boil. Add the rice to the other ingredients in the paella pan. Stir in the boiling stock and simmer for about 25 minutes, until the rice has absorbed most of the liquid. Stir in the strips of red pepper. Check the seasoning and adjust if necessary.

7 Arrange the chicken pieces, pork, clams and prawns on the rice. Cover the pan with foil and cook in the centre of the oven for a further 15 minutes. Serve straight from the pan, accompanied by wedges of lemon.

Note: Although paella can be made with long-grain rice, the dish's characteristic moist, sticky texture is best achieved by using Spanish rice or a plump, round-grain risotto rice, which should be cooked for as short a time as possible. When serving paella, it is a good idea to provide finger bowls of warm water and slices of lemon, as well as plates for the discarded bones and shells.

A **paella pan** is a large, round, flat-bottomed pan with metal handles. A good alternative is a large fireproof casserole, or a deep frying pan (with a removable handle, if you complete the cooking in the oven). In Spain, paellas are sometimes cooked on an open fire; the flames lick round the edges of the pan, ensuring that the contents are heated evenly. At home, if using a relatively small pan, it is better to finish cooking the paella in the more evenly distributed heat of the oven (*as in Step 7*), not on top of the stove.

Arroz emperado

Rice with white beans

Takes a little time • Catalonia

Serves 4

**150 g dried haricot, or other
white, beans
1 garlic head
¾ litre meat stock
200 mg powdered saffron
1 bay leaf
300 g Spanish round-grain rice
or Italian arborio rice
1 large beef tomato
2 tbsp olive oil
1 tsp mild paprika
salt
freshly ground black pepper**

**Preparation time: 1¼ hours
(plus 12 hours soaking time)**

1,800 kJ/430 calories per portion

1 Soak the beans overnight in cold water. Next day, pour off the water, place the beans in a pan with 1 litre of fresh water, cover, and bring to the boil. Reduce the heat to low and simmer for about 1 hour, until tender.

2 Meanwhile, break off and set aside 4 garlic cloves. Place the rest of the head, unpeeled, in another pan together with the stock and bring to the boil. Add the saffron and the bay leaf. Reduce the heat to low, sprinkle in the rice, cover, and simmer for about 20 minutes, until the liquid is absorbed.

3 Plunge the tomato briefly into boiling water, skin, halve and remove the seeds. Chop into small pieces.

4 Heat the oil in a large pan. Peel the reserved garlic cloves and crush them into the pan. Stir in the paprika and the tomato, and cook for about 5 minutes.

5 Remove the garlic head and bay leaf from the rice. Drain the beans. Add the beans and rice to the large pan. Season generously with salt and pepper, stir thoroughly and serve.

Variation: For a vegetarian main course, use vegetable stock instead of meat stock. You can also sprinkle the cooked rice with Manchego cheese (*see page 75*) and brown it under the grill.

Note: This dish makes a good accompaniment for meat or poultry.

Alcachofas fritas

Fried artichokes

Not difficult • Navarre

Serves 4 to 6

**3 lemons
12 small young artichokes
4 to 6 garlic cloves
6 tbsp olive oil
salt
freshly ground black pepper**

Preparation time: 30 minutes

**510 kJ/180 calories per portion
(if serving 6)**

1 Fill a large bowl with water, and add the juice of one of the lemons.

2 With a sharp knife, cut off the artichoke stalks, leaving a short stump. Remove the tough outer leaves, so that the base is almost exposed, and trim off the tips of the remaining leaves.

3 Wash the artichokes under cold running water to remove any grit, cut them into quarters, and drop into the acidulated water.

4 Peel and thinly slice the garlic. Heat the oil in a large frying pan over medium heat. Remove the artichoke quarters from the water, pat dry and fry

in the hot oil for about 5 minutes. Add the garlic, season with salt and pepper, and continue cooking for a further 5 minutes, until golden.

5 Serve hot, with the remaining lemons cut into wedges.

Note: Very young artichokes have been used in this recipe. If you use slightly older ones, you may need to remove the chokes. Because artichokes react chemically to metals such as aluminium and contact with air discolours their cut edges, use only stainless steel knives and non-reactive pans, and put trimmed artichokes in acidulated water or rub the cut edges with lemon juice.

Espinacas Sacromonte

Not difficult • Granada

Spinach with almonds and raisins

Serves 4

1 kg leaf spinach
100 g almonds
2 slices day-old white bread
5 tbsp olive oil
2 garlic cloves
50 g raisins
salt
freshly ground black pepper
saffron threads

Preparation time: 40 minutes

1,500 kJ/360 calories per portion

1 Trim the spinach, removing the stalks. Wash and drain.

2 Blanch the almonds (*see page 50, Step 1*). Cut the bread into small cubes.

3 In a frying pan, heat 1 tbsp olive oil. Add the blanched almonds and toast until golden-brown. Remove from the pan and set aside. Pour in a further 2 tbsp oil, and fry the bread cubes until crisp. While the bread is frying, peel and crush the garlic into the pan. Transfer the mixture to a mortar or food processor and grind to a paste.

4 In a large, heavy pan, heat the remaining olive oil. Sauté the spinach and raisins for about 5 minutes, until the spinach wilts. Stir in the almond paste and season with salt, pepper and a few saffron threads. Heat through and serve.

Variation: Sauté the spinach with chopped onions, lots of garlic and diced *serrano* ham. Season with salt, pepper and nutmeg. Serve hot or cold.

Note: Serve as a side dish with meat, fish or poultry. With rice, this dish makes a good vegetarian main course.

Pisto manchego

Simple • La Mancha

Vegetable ragout

Serves 4

750 g ripe beef tomatoes
1 large onion
3 garlic cloves
2 sweet green peppers
(about 300 g)
500 g courgettes
3 tbsp olive oil
salt
freshly ground black pepper
30 g flat-leaf parsley

Preparation time: 1 hour

650 kJ/150 calories per portion

1 Plunge the tomatoes briefly into boiling water, then skin, halve and deseed them. Coarsely chop the flesh. Peel and finely chop the onion. Peel the garlic.

2 Wash the green peppers. Cut into quarters, remove the seeds and ribs and cut into strips about 2 cm wide. Trim and wash the courgettes. Halve or quarter them lengthwise—depending on their size—and cut into 2 cm lengths.

3 Heat the oil in a pan and sauté the onion until transparent. Crush the garlic cloves into the pan. Stir in the green peppers and the courgettes and sauté briefly.

4 Stir in the tomatoes, and season with salt and pepper. Cook, uncovered, over low heat for about 25 minutes, until almost all the liquid has evaporated.

5 Meanwhile, wash the parsley and shake dry. Tear off the leaves and chop them finely, Shortly before the end of the cooking time, stir the chopped parsley into the vegetables. If there is still too much liquid, increase the heat for the last few minutes.

Note: This dish can be served hot or cold with fish, meat or poultry, or as a vegetarian main course. In small portions it also makes ideal *tapas*.

Escalivada

Simple • Catalonia **Baked mixed vegetables** *Serves 4*

6 tbsp olive oil
2 floury potatoes (about 500 g)
2 medium-sized onions
2 sweet red peppers (about 300 g)
2 small aubergines (about 600 g)
2 medium-sized beef tomatoes
(about 500 g)
juice of ½ lemon
salt
freshly ground black pepper

Preparation time: about 1¼ hours

1,300 kJ/310 calories per portion

1 Preheat the oven to 180°C (350°F or Mark 4). Grease a baking sheet with 2 tbsp olive oil.

2 Wash the potatoes, cut in half lengthwise and lay on the baking sheet, cut side down. Place in the oven.

3 Meanwhile, peel the onions and cut in half crosswise. Wash and halve the red peppers, remove the seeds and ribs, and cut into wide strips. Wash the aubergines and remove the stalks. Slice lengthwise, then cut into strips.

4 When the potatoes have been in the oven for 15 minutes, place the onions on the baking sheet, cut side down. After another 5 minutes, add the peppers and aubergines, and sprinkle with a little of the remaining olive oil.

5 Wash the tomatoes and cut in half crosswise. When the peppers and aubergines have been in the oven for about 20 minutes, turn them over and place the tomatoes on the baking sheet, cut side down. Continue to cook all the vegetables for a further 20 minutes.

6 Mix the remaining olive oil with the lemon juice. Arrange the vegetables on a serving dish, sprinkle with the oil and lemon dressing, and season with salt and pepper. Serve warm or cold.

Wine: A dry white wine from Catalonia goes well with this dish.

Note: *Escalivada* can accompany meat, fish or vegetables, and also makes an excellent vegetarian main course.

Olives and olive oil

The olive, native to the Mediterranean, has been cultivated for its oil and as a food since at least 3000 BC. Today, about 90 per cent of the world's olive production is used to make oil, with the rest of the fruit—inedible when raw—being cured and treated for the table. Spain is the world's largest producer, and major exporter, of table olives—green (half-ripe) or black (ripe), whole or stoned, or stuffed with almonds, anchovies, onions, sweet peppers or capers.

Olives are still often painstakingly picked by hand. They are then sorted, washed and processed as quickly as possible. At the mills, the fruit is first crushed, then pressed, then placed in centrifuges to separate the oil from the olive juices. It takes 4 to 5 kg of ripe fruit to produce a litre of oil.

The best quality oils come from the first cold pressings, and fall into two categories: unrefined extra virgin olive oil and virgin olive oil. Both have a rich, full flavour best suited to cold dishes and sauces, but not for frying. The oil from further, heated pressings is refined, blended and sold as pure, extra fine or fine olive oil. These oils have less flavour and are more suitable for frying. Round the Mediterranean, especially in Italy and Spain, olive oil is used for most cooking, even for deep frying.

Berenjenas Alpujarra

Aubergines Alpujarra-style

4 medium-sized aubergines
(about 1.5 kg)
juice of ½ lemon
2 onions
2½ tbsp olive oil
15 g fresh mint
3 eggs
2 tbsp fresh breadcrumbs
4 tbsp freshly grated Manchego
cheese (see page 75)
salt
freshly ground black pepper
ground cinnamon

Preparation time: 1 hour

1,100 kJ/240 calories per portion

1 Preheat the oven to 180°C (350°F or Mark 4). Put the lemon juice in a large pan of water and bring it to the boil. Wash the aubergines, cut them in half lengthwise and add them to the pan. Reduce the heat and simmer for about 5 minutes.

2 Using a sharp knife, remove most of the flesh from the aubergines (*above*), leaving a case about 2 cm thick. Chop the flesh into small cubes. Pare a little of the skin and flesh from the underside of each aubergine case, so that they do not tip over when stuffed.

3 Peel and finely chop the onions. Heat 2 tbsp of the oil in a frying pan and sauté the onions until soft. Add the chopped aubergine flesh to the pan and cook for a further 10 minutes. Transfer to a bowl and leave to cool.

4 Wash the mint and shake dry. Tear off the leaves, chop them finely and add to the onion and aubergine mixture. Add the eggs, breadcrumbs and 3 tbsp of the grated Manchego cheese, and stir thoroughly. Season with plenty of salt, pepper and ground cinnamon.

5 Grease an ovenproof dish with the remaining oil and arrange the aubergine cases in a single layer in the dish. Divide the mixture between the cases (*above*), then sprinkle with the rest of the cheese. Bake in the centre of the oven for 15 to 20 minutes, until golden-brown. Serve with salad.

Wine: A light rosé from Navarre goes particularly well with this dish.

Variation: For the filling, instead of the aubergine flesh you can use 600 g minced meat, which is cooked with the onions (*Step 3*). The chopped aubergine flesh can then be stewed with 2 skinned, chopped beef tomatoes and the mixture puréed and served as a sauce.

Calabacines al horno

Not difficult • Murcia   **Baked courgettes**   *Serves 4*

1 large onion
3 garlic cloves
5½ tbsp olive oil
600 g beef tomatoes
salt
freshly ground black pepper
1 tsp mild paprika
fresh thyme
1 kg courgettes
flour for coating
100 g freshly grated Manchego cheese

Preparation time: 1 hour

1,100 kJ/260 calories per portion

1 Peel and finely chop the onion and the garlic. Heat 2 tbsp of the oil in a frying pan over medium heat, and sauté the onion and garlic until soft.

2 Meanwhile, plunge the tomatoes briefly into boiling water, skin, halve and deseed. Chop the flesh and add it to the frying pan. Season with salt, pepper, the paprika and thyme leaves. Continue to cook, uncovered, over low heat for about 5 minutes.

3 Preheat the oven to 200°C (400°F or Mark 6). Wash and trim the courgettes, and cut them crosswise into slices about 5 mm thick. Season with salt and pepper, and coat with flour. In a frying pan, heat 3 tbsp of the oil over medium

heat and fry the courgettes until golden-brown. Remove from the pan and drain on kitchen paper.

4 Grease an ovenproof dish with the remaining oil. Arrange the courgettes on the bottom, pour over the tomato sauce and sprinkle with the grated cheese. Bake in the centre of the oven for about 15 minutes, until golden-brown. Serve accompanied by potatoes.

Wine: Choose a robust red wine from Penedés to accompany this dish.

Note: This is delicious on its own or as an accompaniment to meat dishes; if serving as a side dish with a main course, the quantities given above are enough for eight people.

Manchego

Don Quixote's native land, La Mancha, is also the home of *queso manchego*, Spain's most famous cheese. Manchego ewes have been bred in the region for centuries, and their milk, rich in fat, retains the taste of the grass and wild herbs of the bleak pastures of La Mancha on which they graze.

Manchego cheese, with its distinctive black or yellow braid-imprinted rind, ranges in texture—like Cheddar—from mild and creamy to hard and crumbly. Shaped into cylinders, it is left to ripen for two to 12 months and is available at several different stages of maturity, from the fresh, pale yellow *tierno* and the delicately flavoured *semi-seco* to the dry, deeply coloured, mature *seco* with a taste reminiscent of good-quality Parmesan. *Anjejos*, as the year-old cheese is known, has the strongest flavour. There is also a variety cured in olive oil for several months.

A favourite with connoisseurs, it is much used in Spanish cuisine: as *tapas*—served with chorizo or cured ham—grated on savoury dishes or as a dessert with quince jam.

Manchego, and a variety of other Spanish cheeses, is increasingly available from good cheese counters and specialist shops.

Tortilla de patatas

Not difficult • Many regions

Potato omelette

Serves 4 to 6

750 g floury potatoes
2 large onions
7 tbsp olive oil
salt
freshly ground black pepper
6 eggs

Preparation time: 1 hour

1,500 kJ/360 calories per portion
(if serving 6)

1 Peel and wash the potatoes, and cut them into thin slices. Peel the onions and dice.

2 Heat half the olive oil in a deep, heavy frying pan about 20 cm in diameter. Add the potato slices and the chopped onion and cook over medium heat for about 25 minutes, until the potatoes are tender but not brown. Season with salt and pepper. When done, remove from the pan with a slotted spoon and allow to cool a little.

3 Meanwhile, in a bowl, whisk the eggs until foamy and season with plenty of salt and pepper. Carefully stir in the potatoes and onions.

4 Heat the rest of the olive oil in the frying pan over low heat. Add the egg-and-potato mixture (*above*), and cook for about 6 minutes, gently shaking the pan from time to time, until the omelette begins to set.

5 Remove the pan from the heat, and place a flat plate on top of it (*above*).

Holding the plate in place with your hand, invert the pan and the plate and tip the omelette out on to the plate, cooked side uppermost.

6 Carefully slide the omelette back into the pan (*above*), and cook it on the other side, adding a little more oil if necessary, for a further 6 to 8 minutes until cooked through.

7 Cut the omelette into wedges or cubes. Serve warm or cold.

Variation: Diced ham or sliced chorizo can be added to the beaten egg at the same time as the potatoes and onions.

Note: This simple but satisfying classic dish can be served as *tapas* or as a main or in-between course. Served with salad, it makes an ideal light supper for two. It has many variations, and can be made using vegetables, ham or prawns.

Piperrada

Not difficult • Basque Country   **Mixed pepper omelette**   *Serves 4*

**2 medium-sized sweet peppers
(1 red, 1 green)
2 medium-sized beef tomatoes
(about 350 g)
50 g ham
1 large onion
4 garlic cloves
3 tbsp olive oil
salt
freshly ground black pepper
8 eggs**

Preparation time: 45 minutes

1,900 kJ/450 calories per portion

1 Light the grill or preheat the oven to 250°C (475°F or Mark 9). Wash the sweet peppers, wipe dry and remove the skins (*page 34, top recipe, Step 1*). Halve the peppers, remove the ribs and seeds, and cut into narrow strips.

2 Meanwhile, plunge the tomatoes briefly into boiling water, skin, halve and deseed, and finely dice the flesh. Cut the ham into narrow strips. Peel and finely chop the onion and garlic.

3 Heat half the oil in a frying pan over medium heat and sauté the onion, garlic and ham until the onion is soft.

Add the tomatoes and sweet peppers, season with salt and pepper, and sauté for a further 10 minutes until most of the liquid has evaporated. Transfer the mixture to a bowl.

4 Heat the rest of the olive oil in the frying pan. Whisk the eggs, season with salt and pepper and pour into the pan. Cook over low heat for about 3 minutes, stirring from time to time, until the egg begins to set. Spread the vegetable-and-ham mixture over the egg, cover the pan, and cook for a further 10 minutes, until set. Serve hot with crusty white bread.

Huevos a la flamenca

Fairly easy • Andalucía **Flamenco eggs** *Serves 4*

250 g floury potatoes
3 tbsp olive oil
1 medium-sized onion
2 garlic cloves
2 sweet peppers (1 red, 1 green)
150 g serrano ham (or, if unavailable, prosciutto)
1 chorizo, about 150 g (see page 56)
500 g beef tomatoes
200 g freshly shelled peas
salt
freshly ground black pepper
1 tsp mild paprika
8 eggs

Preparation time: about 1 hour

2,900 kJ/690 calories per portion

1 Peel and wash the potatoes, then cut into small dice. Heat the olive oil in a large frying pan over medium heat and fry the potatoes for about 5 minutes.

2 Peel and finely chop the onion and the garlic. Wash the sweet peppers and remove the stalks, seeds and ribs, then chop into small dice. Add all the vegetables to the pan.

3 Preheat the oven to 180°C (350°F or Mark 4). Chop the ham into small pieces, slice the chorizo, and add them both to the frying pan. Sauté for about 8 minutes.

4 Plunge the tomatoes into boiling water, then skin, halve and deseed. Coarsely chop the flesh. Add the peas and tomatoes to the pan. Season with salt, pepper and the paprika, stir, and cook for a further 5 minutes.

5 Grease a large baking dish and fill it with the vegetable mixture. Break each egg carefully into the dish and bake in the centre of the oven for about 10 minutes, until the eggs are set. If you like, sprinkle with a little more paprika, and serve with white bread.

Wine: A red or rosé wine from Navarre goes well with this dish.

Note: The combination of vegetables can be varied according to what is in season. If you prefer, you can divide the mixture into 4 dishes and break 2 eggs into each.

79

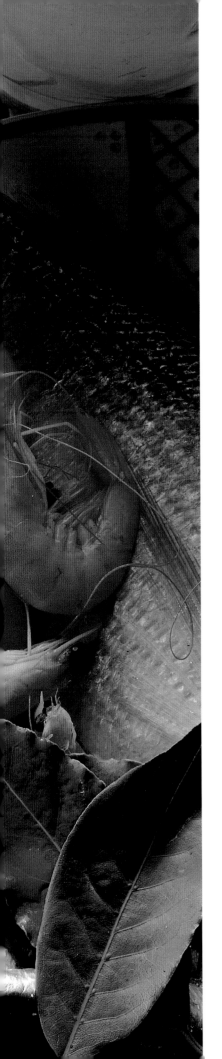

FISH AND SHELLFISH

With a coastline of more than 2,100 kilometres, Spain enjoys a huge variety of fish and shellfish. To the north and west lie the stormy Bay of Biscay and the Atlantic; to the south are the warmer waters of the Mediterranean. Inland, streams and rivers yield delectable freshwater trout.

Regular deliveries from the coast to the bars and restaurants of Madrid testify to the Spanish love of seafood. After the Japanese, they are the world's greatest consumers of fish and shellfish, and in those areas where fresh seafood is less available, dried salt cod—caught in the North Sea—is a popular staple. But this culinary passion for fish reaches its height around the coast, where the freshest possible seafood is available. In inland Spain, fish traditionally appears on a formal menu before the main meat course; on the coast, it often forms a meal in itself, providing *tapas*, soups and main courses.

As a general rule, simple is best. Fish is often served grilled with a little oil or lightly fried. Shellfish, which is usually thought of as an appetizer or first course, is likewise often grilled instead of boiled. As in all Spanish cookery, however, there are many regional specialities which are the subjects of fierce pride and debate: the best scallops, say, come from Galicia; an authentic paella is only made in Valencia; while Catalonia holds the patent on *zarzuela,* a so-called "operetta" of mixed seafood.

Zarzuela de mariscos

Shellfish stew

1 kg beef tomatoes
2 large onions
6 garlic cloves
1 fresh, or dried, chili pepper (see Glossary)
100 g rindless, lean bacon
10 cl olive oil
100 g ground almonds
200 mg powdered saffron
4 bay leaves
1 sprig thyme
1 sprig rosemary
½ litre dry white wine
juice of ½ lemon
salt
freshly ground black pepper
500 g clams
500 g cockles
6 large, fresh, unpeeled prawns
12 cleaned scallops, shells removed
400 g cleaned squid
3 lemons

Preparation time: 1¼ hours

2,400 kJ/570 calories per portion

1 Plunge the tomatoes briefly into boiling water. Skin, halve and deseed them, and coarsely chop the flesh. Peel and finely chop the onions and garlic. Wash the chili pepper. If fresh, deseed and cut into thin rings; if dried, crush with the back of a spoon. Cut the bacon into small dice.

2 In a large saucepan, heat the oil. Sauté the onions, garlic and chili pepper over medium heat, until the onions are transparent. Stir in the bacon. Add the tomatoes, reduce the heat to low, and simmer gently for about 10 minutes.

3 Add the ground almonds, saffron powder, bay leaves, thyme and rosemary to the pan. Pour in the white wine and ½ litre water. Stir in the lemon juice, and season with salt and pepper. Bring to the boil, then reduce the heat to low, cover and simmer for about 15 minutes more.

4 Meanwhile, thoroughly scrub the clams and cockles with a brush under cold running water (*above*). Discard any that are already open.

5 Add the clams and cockles to the other ingredients in the saucepan. Replace the lid and cook until the shells open, about 5 minutes. Discard any that remain closed.

6 Wash and dry the prawns and scallops. Cut the squid into thin rings (*above*) and add together with the prawns and scallops to the pan. Continue to cook, covered, over low heat for a further 10 minutes.

7 Cut the lemons lengthwise into wedges. Check the *zarzuela* for seasoning and adjust if necessary. Serve straight from the cooking pan, with the lemon wedges and crusty white bread.

Wine: A dry, white Penedés from Catalonia goes particularly well with *zarzuela*.

Note: Because guests use their fingers to eat this dish, provide everyone with a small finger bowl of warm water with a lemon slice in it and a large table napkin. *Zarzuela* is also the name for a satirical type of Spanish operetta.

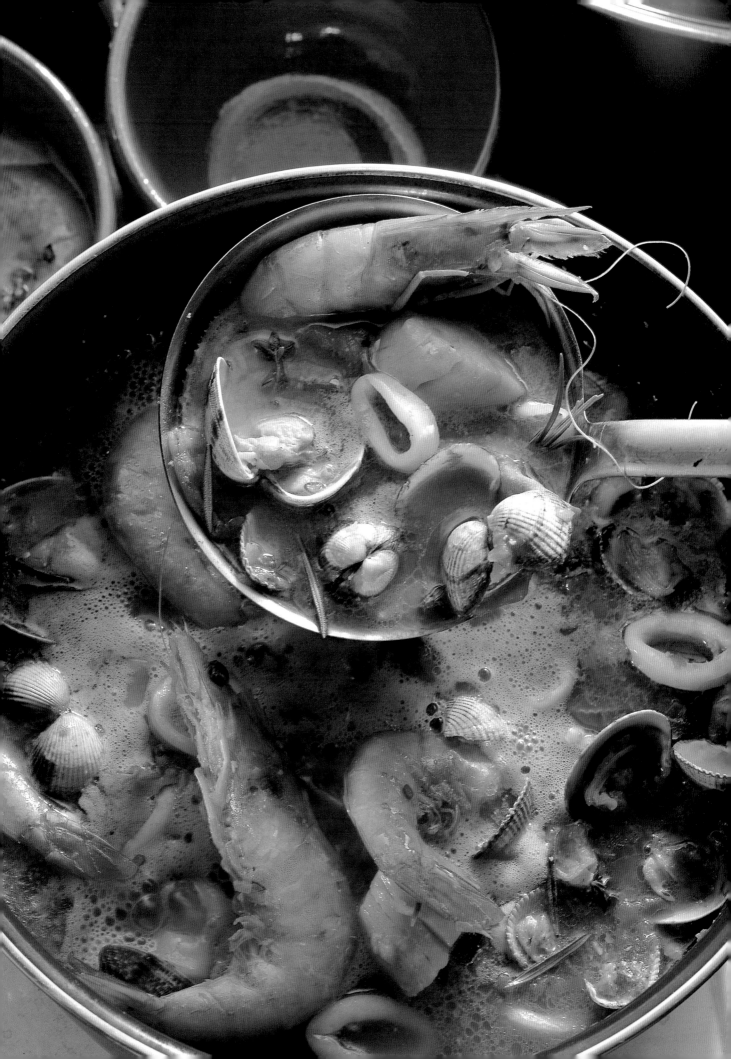

Vieiras a la gallega

Not difficult · Galicia **Baked scallops** *Serves 4*

16 cleaned scallops, including corals
juice of 1 lemon
1 onion
4 tbsp olive oil
2 garlic cloves
4 cl aguardiente de orujo (see Note)
or grappa
1 tsp mild paprika
cayenne pepper
ground cinnamon
salt
freshly ground black pepper
20 cl dry white wine
30 g flat-leaf parsley
4 tbsp fresh breadcrumbs

Preparation time: 45 minutes

1,100 kJ/260 calories per portion

1 Rinse the scallops under running water and pat dry. Separate the white flesh and the pink coral. Finely chop the coral, sprinkle the white flesh with lemon juice and set both aside. Preheat the oven to 200°C (400°F or Mark 6).

2 Peel and finely chop the onion. In a large saucepan, heat 1 tbsp of the olive oil and sauté the onion over medium heat until transparent. Peel and crush the garlic into the onion. Stir in the scallop coral. Pour in the *aguardiente* and season with the paprika, a little cayenne pepper, cinnamon, salt and pepper. Add the white wine, bring to the boil, then remove from the heat.

3 Wash the parsley, shake dry and remove the stalks. Finely chop the leaves and mix with the breadcrumbs. Arrange the scallops in oiled individual shells or in a single layer in an oiled baking dish.

4 Pour the sauce over the scallops and top evenly with the breadcrumb and parsley mixture. Sprinkle with the rest of the oil and bake in the centre of the oven for 10 to 12 minutes, until golden-brown. Serve with crusty white bread.

Wine: A dry white wine from Galicia, goes extremely well with this dish.

Note: When buying fresh scallops—usually sold ready opened and cleaned, attached to the flat half-shell—ask for the rounded top shells, which make attractive individual "dishes". Clean them by scrubbing vigorously with a nailbrush under cold running water. *Aguardiente de orujo* is a strong Spanish spirit distilled from wine skins, similar to grappa and marc.

Lemons

It is hard to imagine Spanish cooking without the lemon. The tart juice enhances the flavour of fish, grilled meat, stews, vegetable dishes and salads. In appetizers, it helps sharpen the appetite; in desserts or drinks, its clean taste refreshes the palate after a meal. Sliced or cut into wedges, it makes a bright, attractive garnish for a wide range of dishes.

The lemon tree, like most citrus fruits, originated in Southeast Asia. It was introduced to North Africa and Spain by the Moors between 1000 and 1200, and later spread all round the Mediterranean, whose

climate was well suited to its cultivation. In Spain, where about 150,000 hectares are given over to lemon orchards, the trees flourish particularly in the southern coastal regions of the Levant—Valencia and Murcia—and Andalucía, and the country is a major exporter.

Lemon trees grow to a height of

between 3 and 6 metres and are characterized by sharp thorns, dark evergreen leaves and fragrant white blossoms. The trees bloom and fruit throughout the year. The juicy yellow fruit is a valuable source of vitamin C, which aids metabolism and strengthens the body's natural defences against disease.

Salmón a la ribereña

Simple • Asturias

Salmon with ham and cider sauce

Serves 4

4 salmon steaks (about 180 g each)
juice of ½ lemon
salt
50 g serrano ham (or, if unavailable, prosciutto)
6 tbsp flour
4 tbsp olive oil
freshly ground white pepper
¼ litre Asturian or other strong dry cider

Preparation time: 45 minutes

1,200 kJ/290 calories per portion

1 Rinse the salmon steaks under cold running water and pat dry. Place in a dish, sprinkle both sides with the lemon juice and season lightly with salt. Leave to marinate for about 15 minutes. Meanwhile, finely dice the ham.

2 Put the flour on a plate and dip the salmon steaks in the flour to coat them, shaking off any surplus flour. Heat the olive oil in a frying pan and fry the salmon over medium heat for about 4 minutes on each side. Season lightly with white pepper, then remove from the pan and keep warm.

3 Sauté the diced ham in the oil remaining in the pan for about 5 minutes. Add the cider and cook over high heat until reduced by about one third. Season with pepper.

4 Arrange the salmon on warmed plates and pour over the sauce. Serve accompanied by spinach.

Note: Asturian cider is the best drink to go with this dish; otherwise, any dry cider, or a white wine, is suitable.

Besugo al horno

Takes a little time • Andalucía

Baked sea bream

Serves 4

1 unwaxed lemon
1 cleaned sea bream (about 1.2 kg)
salt
freshly ground white pepper
600 g small, even-sized floury potatoes
1 onion
4 garlic cloves
1 large beef tomato
2 tsp fresh thyme leaves
10 cl olive oil
¼ litre dry white wine
olive oil
30 g flat-leaf parsley
2 tbsp fresh breadcrumbs

Preparation time: 1½ hours

3,300 kJ/790 calories per portion

1 Scrub the lemon under hot running water. Cut in half lengthwise and cut one half into 4 wedges and set aside. Squeeze the juice from the other half.

2 Rinse the fish, pat dry, sprinkle inside and out with the lemon juice and season with salt and pepper. Make 4 diagonal incisions in the fish with a sharp knife and insert the lemon wedges. Preheat the oven to 180°C (350°F or Mark 4).

3 Peel and thinly slice the potatoes. Peel and halve the onion, and cut into thin rings. Put potatoes and onions in a bowl. Peel the garlic, crush 2 cloves into the bowl and reserve the others.

4 Plunge the tomato briefly into boiling water. Skin, halve and deseed.

Coarsely chop the flesh, and add to the potatoes. Add the thyme, season with salt and pepper, and stir thoroughly.

5 Grease a baking dish with a little of the olive oil and arrange the vegetables on the bottom. Pour over the white wine and the remaining oil. Lay the fish on top.

6 Wash the parsley, shake dry and remove the stalks. Chop the leaves finely and place in a bowl with the breadcrumbs. Crush in the remaining garlic, season with salt and pepper, mix and spread over the fish.

7 Place the dish in the centre of the oven and bake for about 50 minutes. The fish is cooked if firm when pressed with a finger.

Merluza con alcaparras

Hake with caper sauce

Fairly easy • Catalonia

Serves 4

1 garlic head
4 hake steaks (each about 200 g)
salt
freshly ground black pepper
1 tbsp olive oil
20 cl dry white wine
1 small onion
100 g almonds
60 g capers

Preparation time: 45 minutes

1,600 kJ/380 calories per portion

1 Preheat the oven to 180°C (350°F or Mark 4). Place the garlic on a rack or griddle in the centre of the oven and roast for 15 to 20 minutes.

2 Rinse the fish under cold running water, pat dry, and season with salt and pepper. Grease an ovenproof baking dish with the oil, arrange the fish steaks side by side in the bottom, and pour over the white wine. Cover and bake in the centre of the oven for about 20 minutes.

3 Meanwhile, peel and coarsely chop the onion. Blanch the almonds (*see page 50, Step 1*) and toast them in a dry frying pan over low heat until

golden. Carefully peel the garlic cloves and crush them and the almonds, onion and 50 g of the capers, with a pestle and mortar or in a food processor.

4 Remove the fish from the baking dish with a fish slice or slotted spoon and keep warm. Bring the stock left in the dish to the boil, then reduce the heat to low. Stir in the almond paste, season with salt and pepper and continue to cook until hot. Transfer the fish to four serving plates and pour over the sauce. Garnish with the rest of the capers and serve with vegetables.

Wine: A dry white wine from Valencia is excellent with this dish.

Marmitako

Tuna casserole

Fairly easy • Basque Country

Serves 4

1 large onion
4 garlic cloves
1 large sweet red pepper
1 large sweet green pepper
500 g beef tomatoes
2 tbsp olive oil
1 fresh chili pepper (see Glossary)
salt
freshly ground black pepper
2 tsp mild paprika
400 g floury potatoes
¼ litre dry white wine
600 g fresh tuna
juice of 1 lemon

Preparation time: 1½ hours

2,400 kJ/570 calories per portion

1 Peel and finely chop the onion. Peel the garlic. Wash the red and green peppers, halve, remove the ribs and seeds, and cut the flesh into narrow strips. Plunge the tomatoes briefly into boiling water. Skin, halve, deseed and coarsely chop the flesh.

2 Heat the olive oil in a large fireproof casserole or heavy saucepan. Sauté the onion until soft. Crush the garlic into the pan, stir in the peppers and sauté for about 5 minutes more.

3 Wash the chili pepper and deseed it. Cut it into thin strips and add to the casserole. Season with salt and pepper, and the paprika. Stir thoroughly, cover the pan and cook over low heat for about 10 minutes.

4 Peel the potatoes and cut into 1.5 cm dice. Stir the white wine and diced potatoes into the casserole. Cover and simmer over low heat for about 25 minutes.

5 Rinse the tuna under cold running water and pat dry. Cut it into dice the same size as the potatoes. Sprinkle the fish with the lemon juice, season with salt and pepper, and add to the casserole. Cover and cook for a further 5 minutes. Check the seasoning and adjust if necessary. Serve with crusty white bread.

Wine: Serve with a dry white wine from the Basque Country.

Dorada al sal

Not difficult • Andalucía   **Gilt-head bream in a salt crust**   *Serves 4*

*1 cleaned gilt-head bream (about
1.2 kg)*
juice of ½ lemon
salt
freshly ground white pepper
1 sprig thyme
3 garlic cloves
2 kg coarse sea salt
2 unwaxed lemons

For the romesco sauce:
50 g almonds
1 large beef tomato
3 garlic cloves
salt
freshly ground black pepper
cayenne pepper
1 tbsp red wine vinegar
6 tbsp olive oil

Preparation time: 1 hour

2,400 kJ/570 calories per portion

1 Preheat the oven to 250°C (475°F or Mark 9). Rinse the fish thoroughly under cold running water and pat dry. Sprinkle with the lemon juice inside and out, and season with salt and white pepper. Rinse the thyme and pat dry. Peel the garlic and halve each clove lengthwise. Place the thyme and garlic inside the fish (*above*).

2 Pour half the sea salt into a roasting pan or ovenproof dish and spread in an even layer over the bottom. Lay the fish on top.

3 Sprinkle the rest of the salt over the fish, so that it is completely covered (*above*). Place in the centre of the oven and bake for 35 to 40 minutes.

4 Meanwhile, prepare the *romesco* sauce. Blanch the almonds (*Page 50,*

Step 1) and toast them briefly in a dry frying pan until golden (*above*). Plunge the tomato briefly into boiling water; skin, halve and deseed. Peel the garlic. Chop the almonds, tomatoes and garlic finely together in a food processor or vegetable mill.

5 Season with plenty of salt and black pepper, and add some cayenne pepper and the wine vinegar. Stir in the oil.

6 Remove the fish from the oven and break off the salt crust (*above*). Lift the fish carefully out of the dish, skin it and gently pull the flesh away from the bones in fillets. Serve with the *romesco* sauce, the lemons cut into wedges, and accompanied by a side dish of potatoes.

Wine: Choose a dry white wine, such as an Albariño from Galicia.

Truchas a la navarra

Quick and easy • Navarre

Trout stuffed with ham

Serves 4

4 cleaned trout (about 350 g each)
salt
freshly ground black pepper
4 slices (about 150 g) serrano ham
(or, if unavailable, prosciutto)
flour
100 g rindless streaky bacon
5 tbsp olive oil
1 unwaxed lemon

Preparation time: 25 minutes

3,000 kJ/710 calories per portion

1 Rinse the trout under cold running water, pat dry and season lightly inside and out with salt and pepper. Place a folded slice of ham inside each fish.

2 Spread some flour on a plate and turn each trout in the flour to coat it evenly, shaking to remove any excess.

3 Finely dice the bacon. Heat the oil in a frying pan and fry the bacon over low heat until it has rendered up most of its fat.

4 Add the trout to the pan and fry them for about 10 minutes, turning once, until golden-brown all over. Transfer to a warmed serving plate, sprinkle the bacon on top and garnish with the lemon cut into wedges. Serve with potatoes or crusty white bread.

Wine: This dish goes very well with a Navarre rosé.

Variations: If you prefer, serve the trout without sprinkling with the bacon. In Asturias, the serrano ham is omitted.

Bacalao al pil-pil

Fairly easy • Basque Country

Salt cod in olive oil and garlic sauce

Serves 4

600 g dried salt cod (see Glossary)
1 garlic head
30 cl olive oil
1 dried chili pepper (see Glossary)
freshly ground white pepper

Preparation time: 35 minutes
(plus 24 hours soaking time)

5,000 kJ/1,200 calories per portion

1 Soak the salt cod in cold water for at least 24 hours, changing the water three or four times. The fish should roughly double in size.

2 Remove the cod from the water and rinse thoroughly. Bone if necessary, taking care not to damage the skin, and cut into serving portions. Peel and thinly slice the garlic.

3 Heat the oil in a high-sided frying pan or fireproof casserole with handle. Crush the chili pepper with the back of a spoon and add to the pan with the garlic. Fry over low heat until the garlic is golden, then remove both garlic and chili pepper with a slotted spoon, reserve the garlic and discard the chili pepper.

4 Lay the salt cod skin down in the olive oil and cook slowly over low heat for about 20 minutes. Constantly shake the pan, so that the fish juices and the oil combine and thicken into a mayonnaise-like sauce. Lightly season the fish and sauce with white pepper.

5 Transfer the fish and sauce to four warmed plates or earthenware dishes, garnish with the reserved garlic slices and serve immediately, accompanied by potatoes or crusty white bread.

Wine: Choose a dry white wine from the Basque Country.

Note: *Bacalao al pil-pil* is also good served cold.

Almejas a la marinera

Simple • Galicia **Clams fisherman-style** *Serves 4 to 6*

1 small onion
2 garlic cloves
600 g beef tomatoes
2 tbsp olive oil
¼ litre dry white wine
1 bay leaf
salt
freshly ground black pepper
1 kg clams
30 g flat-leaf parsley

Preparation time: 1 hour

720 kJ/170 calories per portion
(if serving 6)

1 Peel and finely chop the onion and garlic. Plunge the tomatoes briefly into boiling water; skin and halve them, deseed, and finely chop the flesh.

2 Heat the olive oil in a large saucepan and sauté the onion and garlic over low heat until the onion is soft. Add the chopped tomatoes, white wine and bay leaf. Season with salt and pepper. Simmer, uncovered, over low heat for about 10 minutes.

3 Meanwhile, thoroughly scrub the clams under cold running water, discarding any that are already open.

4 Add the clams to the pan, cover and cook over high heat for 5 to 8 minutes, shaking the pan from time to time. Discard the bay leaf and any clams that remain closed after cooking.

5 Wash the parsley, shake dry, remove the stalks and chop the leaves finely. Transfer the clams and sauce to a serving dish, sprinkle with the chopped parsley and serve with crusty bread.

Note: Other bivalves such as cockles, mussels or Venus shells can be prepared in the same way.

Tumbet de pescado mallorquín

Fish hotpot

Takes time • Majorca

Serves 4

8 tbsp olive oil
750 g cod fillet
salt
freshly ground black pepper
juice of 1 lemon
12.5 cl dry white wine
2 sweet red peppers (about 300 g)
500 g floury potatoes
2 aubergines (about 400 g)
flour
1 large onion
2 garlic cloves
750 g beef tomatoes
2 bay leaves
ground cinnamon
1 tsp sugar

Preparation time: 1¾ hours

2,200 kJ/520 calories per portion

1 Preheat the oven to 180°C (350°F or Mark 4). Brush an ovenproof dish with a little oil and lay the fish in it. Season with salt and pepper, and sprinkle with the lemon juice and wine. Bake in the oven for about 10 minutes. Remove the fish and reserve the pan juices.

2 Increase the oven temperature to 220°C (425°F or Mark 7) and skin the sweet peppers following instructions in Step 1, top recipe, on page 34. Meanwhile, peel the potatoes and cut them into thin slices. Heat 3 tbsp of the oil in a pan and fry the potatoes for about 5 minutes. Add ¼ litre water, cover and cook over low heat for a further 15 minutes. Drain and reserve.

3 Wash, trim and thickly slice the aubergines. Coat in flour and fry in 3 tbsp of the oil over medium heat until golden-brown on both sides. Season with salt and pepper, and reserve.

4 Peel and finely chop the onion and garlic, heat 2 tbsp of the olive oil in a heavy pan and sauté until the onion is soft. Plunge the tomatoes briefly into boiling water, skin and halve them, deseed and coarsely chop the flesh.

5 Add the tomatoes to the pan and stir in the fish pan juices, the bay leaves, some cinnamon and the sugar. Season with salt and pepper, cover and simmer over medium heat for about 15 minutes. Discard the bay leaves, and purée the rest in a food processor.

6 Oil an ovenproof dish. Arrange half the potatoes on the bottom, then half the fish, aubergines and peppers. Repeat, adding a second layer of potatoes, fish, aubergines and peppers. Pour over the puréed sauce, and bake for about 15 minutes. Serve hot.

Wine: This dish goes well with a white Muscatel from Majorca.

MEAT AND GAME

Roasted, grilled, fried or served as spicy sausages or hearty stews, meat is a mainstay of Spanish cookery. As in other severe upland countries, much of this meat comes from smaller animals such as pigs, goats and sheep; these animals are cheaper to raise than cattle, which require extensive grazing. There is also a good supply of game in the wild.

Historically, lamb played a prominent role under the Moors, who did not eat pork; the pig became popular only when they left. Today, no part of the animal is wasted. Apart from prime cuts, pigs provide trotters, tails and ears as well as many kinds of sausages and hams. This waste-not, want-not attitude is also reflected in the regular appearance of offal such as tripe.

More often than not, meat is simply grilled or roasted, cooking methods that depend for success on tender succulent meat from young animals. Those that provide the renowned lamb and pork roasts of central Spain, for example, are sometimes little more than a few weeks old. Veal is more common than beef, and cows are grazed more for their milk than meat.

Despite the dominance of simple dishes, regional specialities vary widely. In Catalonia, for example, beef may be cooked with chocolate; in Asturias, pork is baked in cider. In whatever way they are prepared, meat dishes are usually served with no more elaborate side dishes than fried potatoes or fresh bread.

Ternera "La Mancha"

Veal and vegetable casserole

Not difficult • La Mancha

Serves 4

4 veal escalopes (about 180 g each)
juice of ½ lemon
salt
freshly ground black pepper
1 large onion
2 sweet green peppers
(about 300 g)
2 medium-sized beef tomatoes
(about 400 g)
3 garlic cloves
4 tbsp olive oil
20 cl meat stock

Preparation time: 1 hour

1,400 kJ/330 calories per portion

1 If necessary, pound the escalopes to flatten them. Sprinkle both sides with the lemon juice, and season with salt and pepper. Cover and leave to stand.

2 Peel and finely chop the onion. Wash the green peppers. Halve them, remove the stalks, ribs and seeds, and very finely dice the flesh. Plunge the tomatoes briefly into boiling water. Skin, halve and deseed them, and finely dice the flesh. Mix together in a bowl with the onion and green peppers.

3 Peel and crush the garlic and stir into the vegetables. Season with plenty of salt and pepper.

4 Arrange half the vegetables in the bottom of a large fireproof casserole. Moisten with a little of the olive oil and some stock. Place the escalopes on top so that they overlap, and cover with the remaining vegetables. Pour over the rest of the oil and stock. Cover, and cook over low heat for about 40 minutes, until the meat is tender. Serve with crusty white bread.

Wine: A light red wine from La Mancha goes particularly well with this dish.

Note: The dish can also be baked in the oven at about 180°C (350°F or Mark 4).

Chuletas al estilo de Aragón

Pork chop and potato bake

Not difficult • Aragón

Serves 4

800 g floury potatoes
2 tbsp olive oil
salt
freshly ground black pepper
30 cl dry white wine
4 pork chops (about 180 g each)
50 g chopped almonds
4 garlic cloves
30 g flat-leaf parsley
2 eggs

Preparation time: 1¼ hours

3,200 kJ/760 calories per portion

1 Peel and wash the potatoes, and cut into 5 mm-thick slices. Brush an ovenproof casserole or roasting pan with half the olive oil. Spread the sliced potatoes in a layer over the bottom of the pan, season with salt and pepper, and pour over the wine.

2 Preheat the oven to 200°C (400°F or Mark 6). Season both sides of the chops with salt and pepper, then lay them on top of the potatoes.

3 Heat the remaining oil in a frying pan and fry the almonds until golden; transfer to a bowl. Peel the garlic and crush it over the almonds. Wash and dry the parsley and remove the stalks; finely chop the leaves. Mix with the almonds and garlic, season with salt and pepper and spread over the chops.

4 Cover the casserole and bake in the centre of the oven for about 45 minutes, or until the potatoes have absorbed all the liquid.

5 Meanwhile, hard boil the eggs for about 10 minutes. Plunge them into cold water, shell them and chop finely. Serve the chops and potatoes hot, sprinkled with the chopped egg.

Wine: Choose a dry white wine.

Estofado a la andaluza

Ragout of beef

Takes time • Andalucía

Serves 4

1 garlic head
800 g boned shoulder of beef
1 large sweet green pepper
2 beef tomatoes (about 300 g)
2 large onions
2 medium-sized carrots
(about 200 g)
2 tsp peppercorns
200 mg saffron
½ tsp ground cinnamon
salt
3 tbsp olive oil
2 bay leaves
12.5 cl dry white wine
4 floury potatoes (about 500 g)
30 g flat-leaf parsley
freshly ground black pepper

Preparation time: 2 hours

2,300 kJ/550 calories per portion

1 Preheat the oven to 200°C (400°F or Mark 6). Reserve 2 cloves of the garlic, and roast the rest in the centre of the oven for about 20 minutes.

2 Meanwhile, cut the meat into 2.5 cm dice. Wash and halve the green pepper, remove the stalk, ribs and seeds and cut into narrow strips. Plunge the tomatoes briefly into boiling water, skin and cut into eighths. Peel the onions and cut into fine half-rings. Peel and slice the carrots. Put the meat and vegetables into a fireproof casserole or heavy pan and stir to mix.

3 Peel the raw garlic cloves and grind them and the peppercorns with a pestle and mortar or in a food processor. Add the saffron and cinnamon. Squeeze the roasted garlic cloves from their skins

and add to the spices. Season with salt and mix into a paste.

4 Mix the paste with 10 cl water and the oil, and add to the casserole with the bay leaves. Pour over the wine, bring to the boil, reduce the heat to low, cover and simmer for about 1½ hours.

5 Peel the potatoes and cut into 2.5 cm dice. Stir into the ragout about 20 minutes before the end of cooking time. Wash the parsley, pat dry, remove the stalks and finely chop the leaves. When the meat is tender, discard the bay leaves. Season with salt and freshly ground pepper and stir in the chopped parsley. Serve with crusty white bread.

Wine: This dish goes well with a strong red wine, such as a Navarre or a Rioja.

Solomillo a la malagueña

Roast loin of pork Málaga-style

Serves 4

2 tbsp olive oil
800 g loin of pork
salt
freshly ground black pepper
20 cl Málaga or other dessert wine
10 cl meat stock
5 cm piece cinnamon stick
50 g Málaga or other raisins
100 g almonds

Preparation time: 1½ hours

2,800 kJ/670 calories per portion

1 Preheat the oven to 180°C (350°F or Mark 4).

2 On top of the stove, heat the olive oil in a large fireproof casserole over high heat, until a haze forms above the surface. Add the meat and sear until brown all over. Remove from the heat. Season with salt and black pepper. Pour over the wine and stock. Add the cinnamon and raisins. Cover the casserole and roast in the centre of the oven for about 1 hour, until tender.

3 Meanwhile, blanch the almonds (*see page 50, Step 1*) and toast in a dry frying pan over medium heat until golden. Reserve half and grind the rest with a pestle and mortar or in a food processor.

4 Remove the meat from the casserole and keep warm. Discard the cinnamon and stir the ground almonds into the pan juices. Bring to the boil on top of the stove, reduce the heat to low and simmer, uncovered, for about 5 minutes, adjusting the seasoning if necessary. Meanwhile, slice the meat and arrange on a serving dish. Pour over the sauce and sprinkle with the reserved almonds. Serve immediately, accompanied by rice and vegetables.

Wine: A dry rosé, such as one from Catalonia, goes well with this dish.

Ternera a la sevillana

Roast veal Seville-style

Not difficult • Andalucía

Serves 4

2 beef tomatoes (about 300 g)
2 large onions
1 garlic clove
800 g boned shoulder of veal
salt
freshly ground black pepper
2 tbsp olive oil
12.5 cl dry white wine
12.5 cl meat stock
5 cm piece cinnamon stick
40 g almond slivers
100 g stoned green olives

Preparation time: 1¾ hours

1,700 kJ/400 calories per portion

1 Plunge the tomatoes briefly into boiling water. Skin and halve them, deseed, and coarsely chop the flesh. Peel and finely chop the onions. Peel the garlic clove and cut in half lengthwise. Preheat the oven to 200°C (400°F or Mark 6).

2 Wash the meat, pat dry, and rub all over with salt and pepper. Heat the oil in a shallow fireproof casserole or roasting pan over high heat and sear the meat until brown all over. Reduce heat to medium, add the onion and garlic to the pan oil and cook until soft.

3 Pour over the white wine and cook until slightly reduced. Add the stock and chopped tomatoes. Season with salt and pepper, and add the cinnamon stick. Cover and roast in the centre of the oven for about 1 hour.

4 In a dry frying pan, toast the almond slivers until golden-brown.

5 Remove the meat from the roasting pan and keep warm. Discard the cinnamon stick and set the roasting pan over low heat. Stir the almonds and olives into the pan juices and simmer for about 5 minutes, adding more seasoning if necessary. Slice the meat onto a warmed serving dish, pour over the sauce and serve, accompanied by saffron rice (*see page 105, Note*).

Rabo de toro a la sevillana

Oxtail stew Seville-style

Takes time • Andalucía

Serves 4

1 large onion
1 small leek
1 large carrot
100 g celeriac
4 garlic cloves
5 tbsp olive oil
1.5 kg oxtail, cut into pieces
2 tbsp tomato purée
¼ litre dry red wine
40 cl meat stock
2 bay leaves
1 sprig thyme • 3 cloves
salt
freshly ground black pepper
3 tbsp dry fino sherry

Preparation time: 3¼ hours

3,200 kJ/760 calories per portion

1 Preheat the oven to 150°C (300°F or Mark 2).

2 Peel and coarsely chop the onion. Trim and wash the leek, and cut into thin rings. Peel the carrot and celeriac, and cut into small pieces. Peel and crush the garlic cloves.

3 Heat the oil in a fireproof casserole over high heat until a haze forms above the surface, then quickly sear the oxtail until brown all over. Add the chopped vegetables and crushed garlic and, stirring, sauté for about 5 minutes.

4 Stir in the tomato purée. Pour over the red wine and the stock. Add the bay leaves, thyme and cloves. Season with salt and pepper. Cover tightly and cook in the centre of the oven for about 2½ hours, or until tender, adding a little water if too much liquid evaporates.

5 Remove the oxtail with a slotted spoon. Discard bones and keep the meat warm. Strain the pan juices through a fine sieve into a saucepan. Stir in the sherry. Place over medium heat and cook, uncovered, until the sauce reduces by about half. Check the seasoning and add more salt and pepper if necessary. Serve the oxtail in the sauce, accompanied by potatoes or crusty white bread.

Wine: A strong red Rioja goes particularly well with this dish.

Lenguas con salsa de granada

Calf's tongue with pomegranate sauce

Takes time • Andalucía   *Serves 4*

**2 small fresh calf's tongues (about
500 g each) or 4 pig's tongues
(about 350 g each)
salt
2 pomegranates (or, if unavailable,
5 to 6 tbsp grenadine syrup)
1 large onion
1 tbsp olive oil
10 cl dry (fino) sherry
20 cl meat stock
freshly ground black pepper**

**Preparation time: about 2 hours
(plus 2¼ hours soaking and cooling
time)**

2,100 kJ/500 calories per portion

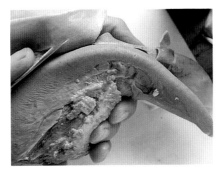

1 Soak the tongues in cold water for about 2 hours, then drain. Transfer to a pan of fresh cold water, bring to the boil to remove impurities and drain.

2 Bring a pan of slightly salted water to the boil, add the tongues, cover and simmer gently over low heat for about 1¼ hours—do not let the liquid boil, as it would toughen the tongues. Cool, then trim off any gristle or fat from the base, loosen the skin with a knife tip and peel off with your fingers (*above*).

3 Meanwhile, cut the pomegranates in half crosswise and scoop out the seeds with a spoon (*above*). Peel and finely chop the onion.

4 Heat the olive oil in a saucepan and sauté the onion until soft. Add the sherry to the pan. Reserve 2 tbsp of the pomegranate seeds and add the rest to the pan. (Or, if using, pour in the grenadine syrup.) Add the stock and simmer for about 20 minutes. Season with salt and black pepper.

5 Slice the tongues across the grain (*above*). Strain the sauce through a sieve into a large saucepan and heat through. Check the seasoning and adjust if necessary. Add the tongues and simmer over low heat for about 15 minutes. Transfer to a warmed serving dish and sprinkle with the reserved pomegranate seeds. Serve with saffron rice (*see Note*).

Wine: Dry sherry or *manzanilla* goes well with this dish.

Variation: Tongue with walnut sauce
Omit the pomegranate sauce and instead simmer 1 chopped garlic clove, 2 skinned, deseeded and chopped tomatoes and 80 g chopped walnuts in 20 cl dry white wine for 20 minutes. Season with salt and pepper, then add the tongue to the sauce as in Step 5.

Note: To make saffron rice, fry 1 small finely chopped onion in 1½ tbsp olive oil in a large, wide pan until soft. Add 300 g round-grain rice and stir for 2 to 3 minutes without browning. Add ¾ litre boiling water, 1 tsp salt and ¼ tsp saffron. Bring back to the boil, stir, then simmer over very low heat until all liquid is absorbed, about 20 minutes. Fluff with a fork before serving.

Cordero a la castellana

Simple but takes time • Castile

Castilian lamb

Serves 4

4 lamb shanks or chump chops
(about 450 g each)
½ litre dry white wine
3 tbsp white wine vinegar
3 bay leaves
1 sprig thyme
1 sprig rosemary
6 juniper berries
1 tsp black peppercorns
1 large onion
4 garlic cloves
2 carrots
1 large beef tomato
salt

Preparation time: 1¾ hours
(plus 12 hours marinating time)

5,000 kJ/1,200 calories per portion

1 Place the lamb shanks or chops in a single layer in dish. Pour over the wine and vinegar to just cover the meat. Add the bay leaves, thyme, rosemary, juniper berries and peppercorns.

2 Peel and finely chop the onion and garlic. Peel the carrots and dice finely. Plunge the tomato briefly into boiling water, skin and halve it, deseed and coarsely chop the flesh. Mix the vegetables together, season with salt, and spread over the lamb.

3 Cover and refrigerate for at least 12 hours, or overnight.

4 When you are ready to cook, transfer the contents of the bowl to a fireproof casserole or heavy saucepan. Bring to the boil, reduce the heat to very low, cover and simmer for about 1½ hours, until tender. Serve the lamb in the pan juices, accompanied by boiled potatoes.

Wine: A dry white wine goes well with this dish.

Variation: If you like, you can add some cooked dried white beans to the other vegetables. Serve with crusty white bread.

Conejo al estilo morisco

Moorish casserole of rabbit

Not difficult • Andalucía

Serves 6

1 rabbit (about 2 kg)
1 kg onions
1 garlic head
5 tbsp olive oil
salt
freshly ground black pepper
200 mg saffron
¼ litre dry white wine
50 g raisins

Preparation time: 1½ hours

3,300 kJ/790 calories per portion

1 Cut the rabbit into 6 portions (or ask the butcher to do it for you). Preheat the oven to 170°C (325°F or Mark 3). Peel the onions and slice into thin rings. Peel and thinly slice the garlic cloves.

2 Heat the olive oil in a fireproof casserole over high heat until a haze forms above the surface. Fry the rabbit pieces until brown all over. Remove from the pan with a slotted spoon, season with plenty of salt and pepper, and set aside.

3 In the fat left in the casserole, sauté the onion over low heat until soft. Remove half and reserve. Spread the remainder out over the bottom of the casserole and place the rabbit pieces on top. Mix the garlic with the rest of the onions and spread over the rabbit.

4 Cover and roast in the centre of the oven for about 20 minutes. Mix the saffron with the white wine and pour over the rabbit. Sprinkle with the raisins. Cover and continue to cook for a further 25 minutes. Serve with crusty white bread.

Variation: Hunter-style rabbit
Cut the rabbit into portions and fry in hot oil until golden-brown. Add 1 chopped onion and 2 chopped garlic cloves. Add a little white wine, 3 coarsely chopped tomatoes, 2 tsp thyme, 1 bay leaf and a sprig of rosemary. Bring to the boil, cover and cook for about 30 minutes. Half way through the cooking time, stir in 250 g halved button mushrooms. Check for seasoning, and serve sprinkled with chopped parsley.

Solomillo de cerdo con jamón

Pork loin with ham

Fairly easy • Extremadura   *Serves 6*

1 kg loin of pork
salt
freshly ground black pepper
1 tsp mild paprika
250 g medium-thick slices serrano ham (or, if unavailable, prosciutto)
500 g pearl onions or shallots
2 tbsp olive oil
10 cl dry (fino) sherry
¼ litre meat stock

Preparation time: about 1½ hours

1,900 kJ/450 calories per portion

1 Rinse the pork under cold running water and pat dry. Mix some salt and pepper with the paprika and rub all over the outside of the meat. Preheat the oven to 180°C (350°F or Mark 4).

2 Lay half the ham slices side by side to form a long rectangle. Place the pork on top and lay the remaining ham over the meat. Wrap the ham in a parcel round the meat and secure with kitchen twine. Peel the onions or shallots.

3 In a roasting pan, heat the oil over high heat until it smokes. Sear the meat parcel until brown all over. Place the onions or shallots round the meat and cook until they begin to brown.

4 Pour over the sherry and the stock. Roast in the centre of the oven for about 1 hour, basting the meat from time to time with the pan juices.

5 Remove the meat from the pan, cut it into slices and arrange on a warmed serving dish with the onions; keep warm. Return the pan juices to the boil, stirring. Add more salt and pepper, if necessary, then pour into a sauceboat. Serve with the meat and onions.

Variation: Instead of wrapping the ham round the meat, dice it and fry in the pan with the onions.

Serrano ham

This finely veined cured ham is one of Spain's most popular delicacies, with a diversity of uses. It lends its characteristic mild taste to a range of dishes throughout the country, both north and south; sliced or in chunks, it is served as a *tapa* with white bread; and the bones give flavour to stocks and stews.

Serrano means "from the sierra", and most ham is produced more than 700 metres above sea level. The ham traditionally comes from the wild, black Iberian pig, which tastes best when it feeds on acorns; today, however, specially bred domestic pigs are more commonly used. The hams are buried in salt for several days or longer, then hung to cure for anything up to a year or more in the cool, fresh air of the mountains.

Because Spanish recipes often call for diced or cubed ham, it is best to buy it in slices at least 3 mm thick. If *serrano* is unavailable, a good substitute is air-dried Italian prosciutto. However, smoked hams, have an entirely different flavour.

Jabalí con higos en Rioja

Fairly easy • La Rioja

Wild boar stewed in red wine

Serves 4

1 medium-sized onion
2 carrots
4 garlic cloves
100 g thick, rindless rashers streaky bacon
800 g leg of wild boar
2 tbsp olive oil
salt
freshly ground black pepper
2 bay leaves
1 sprig fresh, or 1 tsp dried, thyme
1 tsp black peppercorns
2 cloves
2 tbsp sherry vinegar
¼ litre red Rioja wine
¼ litre meat stock
30 g flat-leaf parsley
100 g dried figs

Preparation time: 1¾ hours

3,700 kJ/880 calories per portion

1 Peel the onion and dice finely. Peel the carrots and dice finely. Peel and slice the garlic. Dice the bacon finely. Cut the boar meat into 1.5 cm dice.

2 In a fireproof casserole or heavy pan, heat the olive oil over high heat, until a haze forms over it. Add the meat, in batches if necessary, and brown. Season with salt and freshly ground pepper. Remove from the pan with a slotted spoon and reserve.

3 Fry the bacon in the oil remaining in the pan. Add the onion, carrots and garlic and cook until the vegetables have softened.

4 Return the meat to the pan, add the bay leaves, thyme, peppercorns, cloves and a little salt. Add the sherry vinegar and red wine and enough stock to cover the meat. Slowly bring to the boil, cover, and simmer over low heat for about 1 hour.

5 Meanwhile, wash the parsley and shake dry. Remove the stalks and coarsely chop the leaves. Quarter the figs. About 10 minutes before the end of cooking time, stir the figs and parsley into the stew. Discard the bay leaves and cloves. Serve with potatoes.

Wine: A red Rioja is the best wine to accompany this dish, preferably the one used in the cooking.

Note: Young boar meat is best; meat from older animals can be tough.

Cochifrita a la navarra

Fairly easy • Navarre   **Lamb ragout Navarre-style**   *Serves 4*

1 large onion
1 kg shoulder of lamb
150 g thick, rindless rashers streaky bacon
1 tbsp olive oil
3 garlic cloves
2 tsp mild paprika
1 sprig rosemary
salt
freshly ground black pepper
30 cl Navarre red wine
juice of ½ lemon
30 g flat-leaf parsley

Preparation time: 1¼ hours

1,600 kJ/380 calories per portion

1 Peel and finely chop the onion. Cut the lamb into bite-sized cubes. Finely dice the bacon.

2 In a fireproof casserole or heavy pan, heat the olive oil and slowly cook the bacon until it renders up most of its fat. Add the meat, in batches if necesssary, and brown on all sides.

3 Return all the meat to the pan. Stir in the onion. Peel the garlic, crush into the pan and continue to fry for about 5 minutes until lightly browned. Stir in the paprika, add the rosemary, and season with salt and pepper. Pour in the red wine and simmer, uncovered, until the liquid has reduced by half.

4 Stir the lemon juice into the ragout, cover and continue to cook over low heat for about 20 minutes. Meanwhile, wash the parsley, shake dry, remove the stalks and finely chop the leaves. Discard the rosemary, check the ragout for seasoning and stir in the parsley. Serve with potatoes and green beans.

Wine: A red wine from Navarre goes well with the ragout.

Variation:
Lamb ragout Extremadura-style
Fry the diced lamb over high heat with 1 chopped onion and 8 finely chopped garlic cloves. Add 2 coarsely chopped beef tomatoes, 2 diced sweet peppers, 1 clove and 1 bay leaf. Season with salt, pepper, cumin and paprika. Add just enough water to cover all the ingredients, cover, and cook for about 45 minutes. Soak three slices of white bread in water and stir into the ragout . Before serving, discard the bay leaf and clove, and check the seasoning.

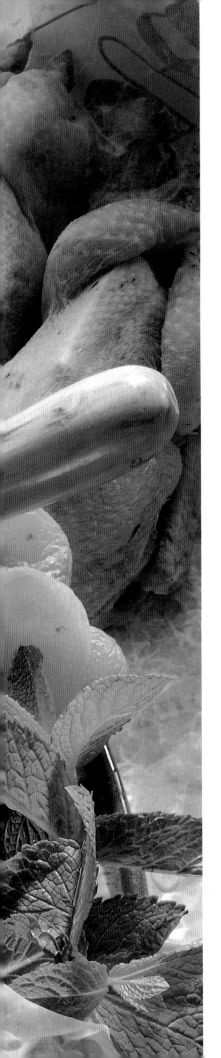

POULTRY AND GAME BIRDS

After fish, Spain's great love is poultry and game birds, which are combined with a wide and unusual range of ingredients—from chocolate, pine-nuts and apricots, to raisins, olives and, of course, sherry.

Chicken is popular nationwide—and has inspired countless simple and more inventive recipes. The delicious aroma of freshly spit-roasted chicken, wafting from little stalls, is a familiar one at Spain's many open-air fairs. At home, however, chicken is seldom cooked whole, but rather grilled or roasted in pieces, in order to better absorb the sauce—whether made with a delicate combination of mint and orange, a robust red wine or a handful of fresh, young garlic cloves. Turkey, too, is popular, especially at Christmas; in Catalonia it is stuffed with a mixture that includes dried fruit, walnuts, pine-nuts, ham or sausage and herbs.

Thanks to its climate and topography, Spain enjoys an abundance of game birds and it is on the main bird migration route to and from Africa. The landlocked, low mountain brushlands of the northeast—Aragón and Navarre— and the wooded uplands of the centre harbour pheasants, partridge and quail; while wild ducks and geese flock to the extensive southern and eastern marshlands.

The cuisine boasts many methods for preparing game birds, especially in the regions where such birds are mostly to be found: Toledo, in particular, is famous for its partridges and Seville for its duck, cooked with the bitter Seville oranges. Today, many birds formerly only to be found in the wild are increasingly farm bred for the table.

Pavo a la catalana

Stuffed roast turkey

Takes time • Catalonia

Serves 6 to 8

100 g stoned prunes
50 g dried apricots
2 tbsp raisins
20 cl amontillado sherry
1 oven-ready turkey, with giblets
(about 3.5 kg)
juice of 1 lemon
salt
freshly ground black pepper
50 g rindless streaky bacon
200 g serrano ham (or, if
unavailable, prosciutto)
80 g pork dripping or good lard
6 raw butifarras (Catalan pork
sausages)
2 apples
2 tbsp pine-nuts
50 g coarsely chopped walnuts
50 g fresh breadcrumbs
1 tsp dried thyme
1 tsp dried oregano
1 sprig rosemary
2 bay leaves
40 cl chicken or turkey stock

Preparation time: 2¾ hours
(plus 1 hour marinating time)

6,100 kJ/1500 calories per portion
(if serving 8)

1 Place the prunes, apricots and raisins in a bowl together with the sherry and leave them to soak for about 1 hour.

2 Remove the giblets from the turkey (*above*), reserve the heart and liver, and discard the rest. Rinse the turkey under cold running water, pat dry and sprinkle inside and out with the lemon juice, salt and pepper.

3 Preheat the oven to 220°C (425°F or Mark 7). Chop the bacon and ham into small pieces. Heat 20 g of the lard in a frying pan over medium heat. Squeeze the sausages out of their skins into the pan, add the ham and bacon and fry until slightly browned. Coarsely chop the heart and liver and add them to the pan. Continue to fry, stirring, for a further 2 minutes. Transfer to a bowl.

4 Peel, quarter, core and slice the apples. Add the apples, pine-nuts and chopped walnuts to the bowl. Drain the prunes, apricots and raisins, reserving the sherry, and add the fruit to the bowl. Add the breadcrumbs and season with the thyme, oregano and plenty of salt and pepper. Stir thoroughly.

5 Stuff the turkey with the mixture, then sew up the body cavity with kitchen twine (*above*). In a large roasting pan, heat the rest of the lard. Sear the turkey in the fat over high heat for about 10 minutes, turning occasionally, until brown all over.

6 Place the turkey in the pan, breast upwards. Lay the sprig of rosemary and the bay leaves over the breast and roast in the centre of the oven for about 30 minutes. Lower the temperature to 180°C (350°F or Mark 4), pour the reserved sherry and the stock over the turkey and continue to roast for about 45 minutes, basting with the pan juices from time to time.

7 Turn off the oven and leave the turkey in it to stand for a further 25 minutes. Remove from the roasting pan and place on a serving dish. Meanwhile, over medium heat, cook the sauce to reduce it and check the seasoning. Carve the turkey, and serve with the stuffing and sauce, accompanied by potatoes and leaf spinach sprinkled, if you like, with raisins and pine-nuts.

Note: This traditional Catalonian way of cooking turkey is a popular dish at Christmas.

Pollo con naranja y menta

Not difficult • Seville — **Chicken breasts with minty orange sauce** — *Serves 4*

2 medium-sized unwaxed oranges
2 tbsp olive oil
4 skinned chicken breasts (about 200 g each)
salt
freshly ground black pepper
6 tbsp amontillado sherry
12.5 cl chicken stock
15 g fresh mint

Preparation time: 1 hour

1,200 kJ/290 calories per portion

1 Scrub the oranges under hot running water. Pare the rind (without the pith) from one orange, cut into very thin strips and reserve. Cut both oranges in half crosswise. Cut one of the unpeeled halves into slices and squeeze the juice of the remaining three.

2 Heat the oil in a deep frying pan over high heat and fry the chicken breasts for about 6 minutes, turning once. Transfer them to a dish, season with salt and pepper, and keep warm.

3 Pour off the fat from the pan. Pour in the sherry and cook briefly, stirring to free any residues in the pan. Add the strips of orange peel and the juice, and the stock. Cook the sauce over high heat until reduced by about one third.

4 Rinse the mint under cold running water and shake dry. Reserve a few small sprigs for decoration, and tear off the rest of the leaves. Finely chop the leaves and stir them into the sauce. Season with salt and pepper. Place the chicken breasts in the sauce, cover the pan, and simmer for about 10 minutes until cooked through.

5 Arrange the chicken on a serving dish. Pour over the sauce, and garnish with the mint sprigs and orange slices. Serve, if you like, on a bed of saffron rice (*see page 105, Note*).

Wine: A rosé from Catalonia is a good accompaniment to this dish.

Sherry

This famous wine, one of the world's oldest, derives its name from the Andalucían city of Jerez de la Frontera, in southwest Spain. It owes its distinctive flavour and fine quality to the region's chalky soil, exceptional climate and a form of yeast, known as *flor* and unique to Jerez, that aids fermentation.

The traditional method by which sherry is matured and blended is known as the *solera* system. The *solera* comprises anything from 20 to 100 kegs stacked in a tier up to five rows high. The youngest sherries are at the top; the oldest, dating from the 19th century, at the bottom. When the fully matured sherry is drawn off at the bottom, the barrel is filled from the one above, and so on up the stack until space is left in the top barrel for the new year's wine. In this way, the sherry is continually blended, thus eliminating vintages and maintaining a consistently high quality.

There are four basic types of sherry, the driest being the pale fino and manzilla, best drunk chilled as an aperitif. The darker amontillado is less dry, but also suitable before a meal. The deep amber oloroso and cream sherries, served at room temperature, are an ideal choice to accompany desserts.

Pollo a la campesina

Country-style chicken

Not difficult · Aragón

Serves 4

500 g beef tomatoes
2 large sweet red peppers (about 350 g)
1 oven-ready chicken (about 1.2 kg)
3 tbsp olive oil
salt · freshly ground black pepper
1 tsp medium-hot paprika
4 garlic cloves
¼ litre dry white wine
1 small dried chili pepper (see Glossary)
1 sprig thyme · 1 bay leaf
100 g olives, stuffed with sweet peppers

Preparation time: 1½ hours

2,500 kJ/600 calories per portion

1 Preheat the oven to 250°C (475°F or Mark 9). Plunge the tomatoes briefly in boiling water, skin and cut into eighths. Skin the sweet peppers (*page 34, top recipe, Step 1*), then halve, remove the stalks, seeds and ribs, and cut the flesh into strips. Reduce oven temperature to 180°C (350°F or Mark 4).

2 Divide the chicken into 8 pieces. Heat the oil in a fireproof casserole over medium heat. Add the chicken pieces and fry until lightly browned. Season with salt, pepper and the paprika. Peel the garlic, crush the flesh and add to the casserole.

3 Pour over the wine, and add the chili pepper, thyme, bay leaf, tomatoes and sweet peppers. Cover the casserole, and cook in the centre of the oven for about 50 minutes.

4 About 10 minutes before the end of the cooking time, slice the olives and stir them into the casserole. Serve the chicken straight from the casserole, with crusty white bread.

Wine: A dry white wine goes best with this dish.

Note: If you prefer, buy 8 chicken portions or ask your butcher to cut the chicken for you.

Pollo al ajillo

Garlic chicken

Not difficult · Many regions

Serves 4

1 oven-ready chicken (about 1.5 kg)
1 garlic head
5 tbsp olive oil
salt
freshly ground black pepper
1 tsp medium-hot paprika
¼ litre dry white wine
2 bay leaves
30 g flat-leaf parsley

Preparation time: about 1 hour

2,800 kJ/670 calories per portion

1 Preheat the oven to 180°C (350°F or Mark 4). Divide the chicken into 8 pieces. Break off the garlic cloves, peel and slice them.

2 Heat the oil in a fireproof casserole over medium heat and fry the chicken pieces, in 2 batches if necessary, until lightly browned. Season with salt, pepper and the paprika, then remove and keep warm.

3 Add the garlic to the remaining fat in the casserole and sauté over low heat, until softened. Add the wine and the bay leaves and bring to the boil.

4 Return the chicken pieces to the casserole, cover, and cook in the centre of the oven for about 40 minutes. Meanwhile, wash the parsley, shake dry and chop fairly coarsely. Serve the chicken straight from the casserole, sprinkled with the parsley and accompanied by crusty white bread— good for mopping up the garlic sauce.

Wine: A dry white wine from Galicia, such as Albariño, goes particularly well with this dish.

Note: This dish is best cooked with young, fresh garlic.

Pollo a la vasca

Fairly easy • Basque Country · **Chicken casserole Basque-style** · *Serves 4*

300 g shallots
2 large sweet red peppers (about 350 g)
100 g serrano ham (or, if unavailable, prosciutto)
4 medium-sized sweet green peppers (about 600 g)
4 garlic cloves
1 oven-ready chicken (about 1.2 kg)
3 tbsp pork dripping or lard
salt
freshly ground black pepper
4 tbsp tomato purée
¼ litre dry white wine

Preparation time: 1 ½ hours

2,900 kJ/690 calories per portion

1 Preheat the oven to 250°C (475°F or Mark 9). Peel the shallots. Skin the red peppers (*page 34, top recipe, Step 1*). Reduce the oven temperature to 180°C (350°F or Mark 4). Halve the red peppers, remove the seeds and ribs, and cut the flesh into narrow strips.

2 Dice the ham. Wash the green peppers, remove the stalks, seeds and ribs, and cut into narrow strips. Peel the garlic.

3 Divide the chicken into 8 pieces. Heat the dripping or lard in a fireproof casserole, and fry the chicken pieces over medium heat until lightly browned. Season with salt and pepper, remove from the pan and keep warm.

4 Fry the shallots in the remaining fat until lightly browned. Stir in the diced ham and the tomato purée. Crush the garlic flesh and add it to the casserole. Add the wine and the red and green peppers. Arrange the chicken pieces on the bed of vegetables, cover, and cook in the oven for about 50 minutes. Serve with potatoes.

Wine: A dry white Rioja is excellent with this dish.

Pintada con albaricoques

Guinea fowl with apricots

More complex • Catalonia

Serves 4

1 large onion
2 carrots
2 small oven-ready guinea fowl
(about 550 g each)
salt
freshly ground black pepper
3 tbsp olive oil
2 garlic cloves
3 tbsp Spanish brandy
5 cm piece cinnamon stick
2 bay leaves
1 sprig fresh, or 1 tsp dried, thyme
30 g flat-leaf parsley
40 cl chicken stock
300 g fresh, or 200 g dried, apricots
50 g pine-nuts
1 to 2 tsp red wine vinegar

Preparation time: 1¾ hours

1,700 kJ/400 calories per portion

1 Peel and finely chop the onion. Peel and slice the carrots. Season the guinea fowl inside and out with salt and pepper, and truss them with kitchen twine (*see Glossary*).

2 Preheat the oven to 180°C (350°F or Mark 4). Heat the oil in a fireproof casserole over medium heat and fry the guinea fowl until lightly browned. Add the onion and the carrots and sauté for about 5 minutes. Peel the garlic, crush the flesh, and add it to the pan.

3 Pour over the brandy, and add the cinnamon stick, bay leaves, thyme and parsley. Pour on the stock, cover the casserole, and roast in the centre of the oven for about 30 minutes.

4 If using fresh apricots, plunge them briefly in boiling water, rinse with ice-cold water, then peel and stone. After the guinea fowl have been in the oven for about 30 minutes, add the apricots (fresh or dried). Return to the oven and cook for a further 25 minutes. Meanwhile, in a dry frying pan, toast the pine-nuts until golden-brown.

5 Remove the guinea fowl from the casserole and keep warm. Discard the bay leaves, cinnamon stick, fresh thyme, if using, and parsley. Purée the sauce in a food processor, return to the casserole and reduce to thicken. Season with salt, pepper and the vinegar.

6 Untruss the guinea fowl. Carve and arrange on a serving dish, and sprinkle with the pine-nuts. Serve, accompanied by rice and the sauce.

Pato a la sevillana

Roast duck with orange and olive sauce

Takes a little time • Seville

Serves 4

1 oven-ready duck (about 1.8 kg)
salt
freshly ground black pepper
1 large onion
4 garlic cloves
2 carrots
1 unwaxed orange
3 tbsp olive oil
1 tbsp flour
1 bay leaf
1 small dried chili pepper
½ litre dry white wine
200 g stoned green olives
sugar
1 tbsp white wine vinegar

Preparation time: 2 hours

5,500 kJ/1300 calories per portion

1 Preheat the oven to 250°C (475°F or Mark 9). Rinse the duck under cold water and pat dry. Season it inside and out with salt and pepper (*above*).

2 Peel and finely chop the onion and the garlic. Peel and slice the carrots. Scrub the orange under hot running water, then cut into slices crosswise.

3 Heat the oil in a roasting pan or large, shallow fireproof casserole over medium heat. Add the duck and fry it on all sides until brown all over. Add the onion, garlic and carrots to the pan, and sauté briefly. Stir in the flour. Add the bay leaf, chili pepper and orange slices.

4 Place in the centre of the oven and roast the duck for about 20 minutes. Reduce the oven temperature to 200°C (400°F or Mark 6), pour over the wine, and cook for a further 45 to 50 minutes, or until done.

5 Remove the duck from the pan and turn off the oven. Place the duck on a rack in another pan and leave to stand in the cooling oven for about 15 minutes. Meanwhile, slice the olives.

6 Remove the bay leaf, chili and the orange slices from the roasting pan, and, over medium heat, reduce the sauce by one third. Season with salt, pepper, a little sugar and the wine vinegar. Sprinkle the olives into the sauce, and heat through.

7 Carve the duck into serving portions (*above*) and arrange on a warmed dish. Serve accompanied by the sauce and boiled potatoes.

Wine: A full-bodied red wine, such as a Rioja, goes well with this dish.

Variation: Instead of oranges and olives, use 6 to 8 fresh figs cut into quarters. Or, cook the duck with a quince paste or jelly, which gives it a really distinctive flavour.

Note: This dish is traditionally cooked with bitter Seville oranges, usually available between the end of December and early February. If you are cooking for only two people, it is easier to buy ready prepared duck breasts.

Codornices emborrachados

Needs a little care • Castille

Quail in wine and brandy sauce

Serves 2 to 4

4 oven-ready quail (about 300 g each)
1 medium-sized onion
50 g serrano ham (or, if unavailable, prosciutto)
4 tbsp olive oil
salt
freshly ground black pepper
3 tbsp Spanish brandy
½ litre dry white wine
10 cl cream

Preparation time: 1 hour

3,000 kJ/710 calories per portion (if serving 4)

1 Cut the quail in half lengthwise. Finely chop the onion. Dice the ham.

2 Heat the oil in a fireproof casserole or sauté pan over medium heat and lightly brown the quail on both sides. Remove from the pan and season with salt and pepper.

3 Add the onion and the ham to the remaining fat, and sauté over low heat for about 3 minutes. Add the brandy and the wine and bring to the boil.

4 Return the quail to the pan, cover and cook over low heat for about 30 minutes. Transfer the quail to a serving dish and keep warm. Add the cream to the sauce, then continue to cook, uncovered, until reduced by about a third. Season with salt and pepper. Pour the sauce over the quail, and serve, accompanied by rice or potatoes.

Variation: Quail in chocolate sauce
Fry the halved quail in oil until golden-brown, season, remove from the pan and keep warm. Sauté 1 chopped onion and 2 chopped garlic cloves until soft. Add ¼ litre red wine, cover and simmer for about 15 minutes. Return the quail to the pan and simmer for about 8 minutes. Remove the quail and keep warm. Stir 3 tbsp red wine vinegar and 3 tbsp grated plain chocolate into the pan liquid. Heat through slowly until the chocolate melts and the sauce thickens. Pour over the quail and serve.

Pichones a la toledana

Fairly easy • Toledo

Toledo-style pigeons

Serves 4

2 onions
5 garlic cloves
4 oven-ready pigeons (about 300 g each)
4 tbsp olive oil
salt
freshly ground black pepper
6 tbsp dry sherry
1 tbsp sherry vinegar

Preparation time: 1¼ hours

2,900 kJ/690 calories per portion

1 Peel and finely chop the onions. Leave the garlic cloves unpeeled, but lightly crush them with the back of a spoon.

2 Divide the pigeons into quarters. Heat the oil in a fireproof casserole over medium heat and brown the pigeon pieces. Season with salt and pepper. Add the onions and garlic, then the sherry and vinegar. Cover, and cook over low heat for about 40 minutes, adding a little water if too dry.

3 Remove the meat from the casserole and keep warm. Cook over high heat for about 3 minutes, to reduce the sauce.

Check the seasoning and adjust if necessary, then strain the sauce. Serve the pigeon, accompanied by the sauce and crusty white bread.

Drink: A dry *fino* sherry goes particularly well with this dish.

Variation: To make a more substantial version of this dish, you can add the coarsely chopped flesh of 3 skinned, deseeded beef tomatoes, and 100 g stoned green olives.

Note: You can substitute dry white wine for the sherry, in which case serve the same white wine with the meal.

DESSERTS AND PASTRIES

With a year-round assortment of delicious produce from which to choose, one of the Spaniards' favourite ways of rounding off a meal is fresh fruit: in spring, a bowl of sweet strawberries from Catalonia; on a hot August day, a slice of ice-cool melon from Murcia; in December, a juicy, freshly picked orange from Valencia.

In addition to its store of natural riches, Spain also boasts a variety of enticing puddings. The culinary influence of the Moors pervades much of the cuisine, nowhere more so than in dessert making, where there is a pronounced use of egg yolks, honey and almonds. Marzipan is of Moorish origin, as is *turrón,* the famous Jijona and Alicante nougat.

In the days when egg whites were widely used to clarify sherry, the leftover yolks were donated to convents, where the nuns transformed them into a variety of exquisite sweetmeats such as *yemas,* candied yolks, or *Tocino de cielo,* a rich caramel custard made from only sugar and egg yolks. Today, continuing the centuries-old tradition, many people in Andalucía still order desserts, sweets and pastries from their local convent for festivities at Christmas or Easter, or to celebrate saints' days.

Torta de almendras
Almond tart

Not difficult • Andalucía

Serves 8 to 12

For the pastry:
200 g flour
100 g butter
50 g sugar
1 egg
1 tbsp milk

For the filling:
150 g almonds
4 eggs
50 g sugar
4 tbsp cream sherry
grated rind of 1 unwaxed lemon
salt

Preparation time: 1½ hours

1,300 kJ/310 calories per portion (if serving 12)

1 Sift the flour into a bowl and make a well in the centre. Dice the butter and add it to the well, together with the sugar. Rub together with your fingers until the mixture has a coarse, mealy texture. Make another well, add the egg and the milk, and stir with a knife until the mixture coheres. Gently knead the dough into a ball, wrap in foil or plastic film and chill for about 30 minutes.

2 For the filling, blanch the almonds (*page 50, Step 1*), pat them dry and grind finely in a food processor or with a mortar and pestle. Separate the eggs and reserve the whites. Whisk the yolks together with the sugar, until frothy. Stir in the ground almonds, sherry and the grated lemon rind.

3 Preheat the oven to 220°C (425°F or Mark 7). Whisk the egg whites and a little salt until the whites form stiff peaks. Fold the egg whites evenly into the egg-and-almond mixture.

4 Grease a 26 cm springform or other cake tin. On a floured work surface, roll out the pastry. Carefully line the tin with the pastry, making the rim about 3 cm high. Fill the case with the almond paste and level the surface.

5 Bake in the centre of the oven for about 30 minutes. If the top begins to brown too quickly, cover it with aluminium foil. Remove the tart from the oven and leave to cool on a wire rack. Serve, if you like, with cream.

Almonds

The almond, one of the most popular and common nuts, is the edible seed of a small fruit closely related to the plum and the peach. Native to Asia and first cultivated in Europe by the Greeks, almonds were introduced to Spain by the Moors. Spain is today among the world's leading exporters of almonds; across its countryside the trees—a mass of white blooms when in flower—are a familar sight.

There are two basic types of almond: the sweet, edible variety, which contains 50 to 60 per cent oil; and the bitter variety—never eaten raw—whose essential oil is used in the manufacture of flavouring extracts.

Almonds can be bought unpeeled, blanched, chopped, flaked or ground. Where a recipe calls for blanched almonds, it is better to buy unpeeled ones and blanch them yourself, because the almonds' thin brown skin preserves the freshness and flavour.

Raw or cooked, almonds are very popular in Spanish cuisine, lending a distinctive flavour to soups, sauces, seafood dishes, pastries and sweets—such as marzipan and the famous nougat, *turrón*.

Flao

Fairly easy • Ibiza   **Cheesecake**

Serves 8 to 12

300 g flour
salt
4 tbsp Spanish anis, or other anise-flavoured liqueur
4 tbsp olive oil
4 eggs
175 g sugar
400 g cream or curd cheese or quark
30 g fresh mint
icing sugar

Preparation time: 1 hour 10 minutes

1,300 kJ/310 calories per portion (if serving 12)

1 Sift the flour into a bowl. Add the salt, liqueur, olive oil and 4 tbsp water and mix together. Knead into a smooth dough and shape into a ball. Cover and leave to stand for about 30 minutes in a cool place.

2 Meanwhile, whisk together the eggs and sugar, until creamy. Mash the cheese thoroughly with a fork, then stir into the eggs and sugar with the whisk.

3 Preheat the oven to 220°C (425°F or Mark 7). Wash the mint and pat dry. Tear off the leaves, chop them coarsely and stir into the filling.

4 Grease a 26 cm springform or other cake tin. Roll the pastry out thinly and line the tin, making an edge about 4 cm high. Pour the filling into the case and level the surface.

5 Bake in the centre of the oven for 30 to 40 minutes, until set. When cooked, leave the cheesecake to cool on a wire cooling rack. Before serving, sprinkle with a little icing sugar.

Note: In Ibiza, this cheesecake is traditionally made with fresh, white ewe's-milk cheese.

Turrón de Jijona

Fairly easy • Alicante   **Almond nougat**

Makes about 25 slices

620 g almonds
400 g icing sugar
100 g clear honey
2 egg whites

Preparation time: 20 minutes (plus 1 week drying-out time)

960 kJ/230 calories per slice

1 Blanch the almonds (*page 50, Step 1*) and wipe them dry. In a dry frying pan, toast the almonds until golden, stirring constantly. Set aside about 70 g whole almonds and finely grind the remainder.

2 Reserve 20 whole almonds and place the rest in a bowl together with the ground almonds and the icing sugar. Add the honey, then the egg whites, and stir thoroughly to form a thick paste.

3 Shape the almond paste into bars about 6 cm wide and 20 cm long. Lay the bars on a sheet of greaseproof paper, decorate with the reserved whole almonds and leave in a cool place for about 1 week to dry out.

4 Cut the nougat into slices and serve.

Note: This celebrated nougat, traditionally a Christmas sweetmeat, is delicious served with coffee after a meal, or simply as a treat. Be sure to use fresh eggs from a source you trust for this recipe, as raw eggs can contain the salmonella bacteria that causes food poisoning.

Leche frita

Custard fritters

4 eggs
140 g butter
250 g flour
120 g sugar
¼ litre milk
5 cm piece cinnamon stick
1 piece unwaxed lemon rind
1 piece unwaxed orange rind
100 g fresh fine breadcrumbs
8 tbsp olive oil
icing sugar
ground cinnamon

Preparation time: 50 minutes
(plus cooling time)

950 kJ/240 calories per square
480 kJ/120 calories per triangle

1 Separate the eggs; reserve the whites in the refrigerator. Slowly melt the butter in a heavy saucepan. Stir in 200 g of the flour, bring to the boil and stir in the sugar.

2 In another saucepan, heat the milk together with the cinnamon stick, lemon and orange rind. Bring to the boil, then stir into the flour mixture.

3 Remove the pan from the heat and discard the cinnamon stick and the lemon and orange rind. Using a hand whisk, mix in the egg yolks one by one.

4 Oil a rectangular dish, about 30 by 15 cm. Fill with the custard to a depth of about 3 cm. Refrigerate to set for at least 3 hours, preferably overnight.

5 When set, cut the custard into 5 cm squares, or halve again into triangles. Whisk the egg whites. Dip the custard pieces in the remaining flour, then in the beaten egg whites, and coat with the breadcrumbs.

6 Heat the oil in a frying pan over medium heat and fry the coated custard pieces on both sides until golden-brown. Arrange on a serving dish, sprinkle with icing sugar and ground cinnamon, and serve warm or cold.

Note: These fritters are an ideal accompaniment to a compote of berries or other fruit.

Churros

Spanish fritters

Makes about 30 fritters

salt
300 g flour
olive, or other, oil for deep frying
icing sugar

Preparation time: 45 minutes
(plus 10 minutes standing time)

1,200 kJ/290 calories per fritter

1 Bring ½ litre salted water to the boil in a heavy saucepan.

2 Reduce the heat to low, add the flour and stir vigorously with a wooden spoon until the dough forms a ball. Remove from the heat, cover, and leave to stand for about 10 minutes.

3 Heat the oil in a deep pan until it sizzles when a small piece of the dough is dropped in. Transfer the dough to a large piping bag fitted with a wide star nozzle. Squeeze rings of the dough, a few at a time, into the hot oil. Fry until just golden, remove with a slotted spoon and drain on kitchen paper. Repeat until all the dough is used up.

4 Serve immediately, sprinkled with a little icing sugar.

Note: These little fritters, freshly fried, can be bought from stands at any fair or festival in Spain, and are sold by the bag in special *churrería* shops. They are delicious eaten for breakfast, or as a snack after late-night festivities with hot thick drinking chocolate. They can also be served as a simple light dessert.

Crema catalana

Catalan caramel cream

½ litre milk
1 vanilla pod
5 cm piece cinnamon stick
2 eggs
4 egg yolks
80 g sugar

For the caramel topping:
100 g sugar

Preparation time: 50 minutes
(plus 1 ½ hours chilling time)

1,500 kJ/360 calories per portion

1 Pour the milk into a saucepan. Slit open the vanilla pod, scrape out the seeds and add them and the vanilla pod to the milk. Add the cinnamon stick, then bring the milk slowly to the boil. Remove the pan from the heat.

2 Place the eggs and the egg yolks in a bowl together with the sugar and whisk for 10 to 15 minutes, until pale yellow and creamy.

3 Remove the vanilla pod and the cinnamon stick from the milk. Trickle the milk slowly into the egg mixture, stirring constantly (*above*).

4 Place the bowl in a large pan filled with gently boiling water and whisk for about 15 minutes, until the custard thickens.

5 Pour the custard into four individual dishes. Leave to cool, then refrigerate for about 30 minutes.

6 To make the caramel topping, place the sugar in a saucepan together with 12.5 cl water, and simmer over very low heat until it caramelizes but is still liquid. Spoon the hot caramel over the chilled custards (*above*); it will cool to form a firm layer. Return to the refrigerator, and serve well chilled.

Variation: Catalan cream and pears
Make the cream as above but omit the caramel topping. Preheat the oven to 200°C (400°F or Mark 6). Peel, halve and core one pear per person. Place the pears in a baking dish with the juice of 1 medium-sized orange, 20 cl Malaga or medium-sweet sherry, 50 g raisins, 50 g chopped almonds and 2 cloves. Bake in the centre of the oven for about 30 minutes. Serve warm or chilled, accompanied by the custard.

Tocino de cielo

Needs care • Andalucía

"Little bits of heaven"

Serves 4

120 g sugar
8 egg yolks
grated rind of 1 unwaxed lemon
bitter almond oil

Preparation time: 20 minutes
(plus 30 minutes or more chilling time)

1,100 kJ/260 calories per portion

1 In a small saucepan, dissolve the sugar in 12.5 cl water over low heat, stirring, then increase the heat and boil without stirring for about 1 minute to form a thick syrup. Remove from the heat.

2 Whisk the egg yolks and stir them slowly into the sugar syrup, then strain the mixture through a fine sieve. Add the grated lemon rind.

3 Grease 4 ramekins—or one large dish—with a little almond oil, then fill with the mixture.

4 Stand the ramekins in a large, deep pan. Pour in boiling water to about two thirds of the depth of the ramekins and cover. Cook over medium heat for about 10 minutes, then test the custards by gently pressing with your finger—they should feel springy. If not yet set, cook for a few minutes more.

5 Let the custards cool before turning them out. Chill for at least 30 minutes, longer if possible, before serving.

Note: *Tocino de cielo* though similar to *Crema catalana* and the French *crème caramel,* are made without milk.

Bollos de cuajada

Not difficult • Canary Islands

Curd cheese balls

Serves 4 to 6

500 g curd cheese or quark
4 eggs
1 tsp ground cinnamon
grated rind of 1 unwaxed lemon
4 heaped tbsp flour
olive, or other, oil for deep frying
70 g clear honey

Preparation time: 30 minutes
(plus 10 minutes standing time)

960 kJ/230 calories per portion
(if serving 6)

1 Thoroughly drain the curd cheese or quark and mash it with a fork.

2 Whisk the eggs in a bowl. Add the cinnamon, grated lemon rind and curd cheese or quark and work into a thick dough. Sprinkle in half the flour. Cover the bowl and leave the dough to stand for about 10 minutes.

3 With floured hands (using the remaining flour), shape the dough into little balls about the size of walnuts. Heat a generous amount of oil in a deep frying pan over medium heat, and fry the balls until golden-brown. Remove them with a slotted spoon and drain on kitchen paper.

4 Arrange the cheese balls on a warmed serving dish, pour over the honey and serve immediately.

Note: In the Canary Islands, these delicious little cakes are traditionally eaten during the carnival season.

Suggested Menus

Spanish cuisine is enormously versatile; restaurant menus are arranged not by course but, as in this book, by category, allowing you to create a meal to suit your own taste or budget. When planning a menu, bear in mind that many of the *tapas*, and the rice, egg or vegetable dishes, make excellent, inexpensive meals. This selection, put together from recipes featured in the book, contains suggestions to suit every occasion from simple, everyday meals to more elaborate ones suitable for festive occasions. For a *tapas* party, choose a selection of dishes from pages 32 to 47 adding, if you like, *serrano* ham, Manchego cheese, olives, pistachios or salted almonds, and serve them with white bread and chilled sherry.

Everyday menus

Summer salad (*Pipirrana*)	38
Garlic chicken (*Pollo al ajillo*)	118
Peaches poached in red wine*	—
Prawn omelette (*Tortilla de gambas*)	40
Roast loin of pork Málaga-style (*Solomillo a la malagueña*)	101
Saffron rice (*see Note, page 105*) and vegetables	—
Almond tart (*Torta de almendras*)	128
Almond and saffron soup (*Sopa de almendras*)	50
Trout stuffed with ham (*Truchas a la navarra*)	93
Spinach with almonds and raisins (*Espinacas Sacromonte*)	68
Fruit salad*	—

When time is short

Garlic soup (*Sopa de ajo*)	53
Chicken breasts with minty orange sauce (*Pollo con naranja y menta*)	116
Selection of fresh fruit*	—
Chilled grape and almond soup (*Ajo blanco con uvas*)	58
Flamenco eggs (*Huevos a la flamenca*)	79
Ice cream, or Manchego cheese with quince jam*	—
Garlic prawns (*Gambas al ajillo*)	42
Hake with caper sauce (*Merluza con alcaparras*)	88
Green salad*	—
Pears poached in white wine*	—
Chicken in sherry (*Pechuga de pollo en jerez*)	44
Gilt-head bream in a salt crust (*Dorada al sal*)	90
Fried bananas*	—

Mixed pepper omelette (*Piperrada*)	78
Baked scallops (*Vieiras a la gallega*)	84
Ice cream with fruit*	—

Menus for hot summer days

Cold vegetable soup (*Gazpacho*)	58
Calf's tongue with pomegranate sauce (*Lenguas con salsa de granada*)	105
Rice with pine-nuts and raisins*	—
Fruit sorbet*	—
Marinated anchovies (*Boquerones en vinagre*)	47
Garlic soup (*Sopa de ajo*)—served chilled	53
Baked scallops (*Vieiras a la gallega*)	84
Cold rice pudding*	—
Russian salad (*Ensaladilla rusa*)	40
Fish soup (*Caldo de pescado*)	55
Guinea fowl with apricots (*Pintada con albaricoques*)	121
Cheese and fresh fruit*	—
Chilled grape and almond soup (*Ajo blanco con uvas*)	58
Chicken breasts with minty orange sauce (*Pollo con naranja y menta*)	116
Vanilla ice cream*, topped with crumbled almond nougat (*Turrón de Jijona*)	131
Carrot salad (*Ensalada de zanahoria*)	37
Garlic prawns (*Gambas al ajillo*)—double the quantities given in recipe	42
Honeydew melon with cream sherry*	—

Cold-weather menus

Chicken croquettes (*Croquetas de pollo*)	37
Stewed tripe with chorizo (*Callos a la gallega*)	56
Almond tart (*Torta de almendras*)	128
Baked courgettes (*Calabacines al horno*)	74
Stuffed mushrooms (*Champiñones rellenos*)	45
Lentil casserole (*Cazuela de lentejas*)	53
Catalan caramel cream (*Crema catalana*)	134
Kidneys in sherry (*Riñones al jerez*)	34
Russian salad (*Ensaladilla rusa*)	40
Chick-pea and spinach stew (*Potaje de garbanzos*)	60
Almond nougat (*Turrón de Jijona*)	131
Fish soup (*Caldo de pescado*)	55
Pork loin with ham (*Solomillo de cerdo con jamón*)	108
Vegetable ragout (*Pisto manchego*)	68
Fresh oranges*	—

Menus to prepare in advance

Pearl onions in sherry vinegar (*Cebolletas al vinagre de jerez*)	33
Moorish-style kebabs (*Pinchos morunos*)	39
Lentil casserole (*Cazuela de lentejas*)	53
Custard fritters (*Leche frita*)	132
Vegetable ragout (*Pisto manchego*)	68
Country-style chicken (*Pollo a la campesina*)	118
Catalan caramel cream (*Crema catalana*)	134
Baked courgettes (*Calabacines al horno*)	74
Potato omelette (*Tortilla de patatas*)	76
Baked sea bream (*Besugo al horno*)	86
Vanilla ice cream with fresh figs*	—
Almond and saffron soup (*Sopa de almendras*)	50
Oxtail stew Seville-style (*Rabo de toro a la sevillana*)	102
Fruit sorbet*	—
Marinated anchovies (*Boquerones en vinagre*)	47
Veal and vegetable casserole (*Ternera "La Mancha"*)	98
Cheesecake (*Flao*)	131

Vegetarian menus

Russian salad (*Ensaladilla rusa*)	40
Chick-pea and spinach stew (*Potaje de garbanzos*)	60
Aubergines Alpujarra-style (*Berenjenas Alpujarra*)	72
Fried artichokes (*Alcachofas fritas*)	67
Fresh fruit or cheese*	—
Summer salad (*Pipirrana*)	38
Potato omelette (*Tortilla de patatas*)	76
Baked mixed vegetables (*Escalivada*)	70
Cheesecake (*Flao*)	131
Rye bread with tomatoes and olives*	—
Spinach with almonds and raisins (*Espinacas Sacromonte*)—served with rice	68
Curd cheese balls (*Bollos de cuajada*)	136
Marinated red peppers (*Pimientos en adobo*)	34
Cold vegetable soup (*Gazpacho*)	58
Baked courgettes (*Calabacines al horno*)	74
Apples with sweet sherry or dessert wine*	—

Fish and seafood menus

Garlic prawns (*Gambas al ajillo*)	42
Summer salad (*Pipirrana*)	38
Shellfish stew (*Zarzuela de mariscos*)	82
Almond tart (*Torta de almendras*)	128

Marinated anchovies (*Boquerones en vinagre*)	47
Clams fisherman-style (*Almejas a la marinera*)	94
Salt cod in olive oil and garlic sauce (*Bacalao al pil-pil*)	93
Baked mixed vegetables (*Escalivada*)	70
Catalan caramel cream (*Crema catalana*)	134
Marinated red peppers (*Pimientos en adobo*)	34
Prawn omelette (*Tortilla de gambas*)	40
Fish soup (*Caldo de pescado*)	55
Baked scallops (*Vieiras a la gallega*)	84
Lemon sorbet*	—

Dinner party menus

Meatballs in tomato sauce (*Albóndigas en salsa de tomate*)	37
Garlic soup (*Sopa de ajo*)	53
Chicken and seafood rice (*Paella*)	64
Catalan caramel cream (*Crema catalana*)	134
Chilled grape and almond soup (*Ajo blanco con uvas*)	58
Quail in wine and brandy sauce (*Codornices emborrachados*)—half quail per person as starter	125
Gilt-head bream in a salt crust (*Dorada al sal*)	90
Mixed pepper omelette (*Piperrada*)	78
Curd cheese balls (*Bollos de cuajada*)	136
Tapas with apéritifs:	
Chicken croquettes (*Croquetas de pollo*)	37
Prawn omelette (*Tortilla de gambas*)	40
Marinated red peppers (*Pimientos en adobo*)	34
Olives and salted almonds*	—
Almond and saffron soup (*Sopa de almendras*)	50
Salmon with ham and cider sauce (*Salmón a la ribereña*)	86
Toledo-style pigeons (*Pichones a la toledana*)	125
Mixed salad*	—
"Little bits of heaven" (*Tocino de cielo*)	136

Christmas

Fish soup (*Caldo de pescado*)	55
Baked sea bream (*Besugo al horno*)	86
Stuffed roast turkey (*Pavo a la catalana*)—served with red cabbage or leaf spinach	114
Almond nougat (*Turrón de Jijona*)	131
and/or marzipan and other festive sweetmeats*	—
Coffee and anis or brandy*	

* Indicates either simple dishes such as green salad or poached fruit, for which there are no recipes and no page reference is indicated, or products such as nougat or sorbet, which can be obtained from well-stocked supermarkets or specialist delicatessens.

Glossary

This glossary is intended as a brief guide to some less familiar cookery terms and ingredients, including words and items found on Spanish menus.

Aceite, aceite de oliva: oil, olive oil

Aceitunas: olives (*see page 71*)

Ajo: garlic (*see page 42*)

Alioli: garlic mayonnaise made from garlic, olive oil, egg yolks and lemon juice. Delicious served with grilled fish or meat, with potatoes or coarse rye bread.

Albóndigas: small fried meatballs made from minced meat, fish or chicken, usually served in a sauce as *tapas*

Alcachofa: artichoke

Alcaparra: caper

Almejas: clams. Mainly farmed in Galicia, and often served in a white wine sauce.

Almendra: almond (*see page 128*)

Amontillado: medium-dry sherry, amber-coloured and full-bodied. Less dry than a *fino* sherry, it can be drunk chilled before a meal.

Angulas: silvery, mild-tasting baby eels, often served in a garlic sauce

Anís: Spanish aniseed-flavoured liqueur

Arroz: rice. The starchy round-grained rice produced in the Levante, around Valencia, is the principal ingredient of paella and many other Spanish rice dishes. Italian *aborio* or *vialone* rice can be used instead.

Azafrán: saffron (*see page 50*)

Bacalao: dried salt cod. A Spanish favourite, especially in the north and inland, salt cod has a strong flavour and should soaked for 24 to 36 hours before cooking, to soften it and remove the salt.

Berenjena: aubergine

Besugo: sea bream. Found both in the Atlantic and the Mediterranean, it has firm, white flesh, and is often baked whole, either stuffed or in a sauce.

Blanch: to plunge food into boiling water for a short period. Done for a number of reasons: to facilitate skinning foods such as tomatoes, peaches or almonds; to remove strong flavours; or to soften vegetables before cooking.

Bocadillo: savoury roll or sandwich

Boquerón: fresh anchovy. These little fish are usually served marinated or deep-fried, but can also be grilled.

Café con leche, café solo: coffee with milk, small black coffee

Callos: tripe

Caramelize: to heat sugar, or a food naturally rich in sugar such as fruit, until the sugar turns brown and syrupy

Catalán-style: usually indicates a dish prepared with chocolate, nuts or sausage

Cava: Spanish sparkling wine produced by the *méthode champenoise*; the best make a good alternative to champagne.

Cebolla: onion

Cerdo: pork

Champiñones: mushrooms

Chili peppers: a variety of hot red or green peppers. They contain volatile oils that can irritate the skin and eyes and must be handled with caution. Wash hands immediately after using them. The seeds of the chili are its hottest part; this should be taken into account when using fresh or dried chili peppers.

Chorizo: strongly spiced paprika sausage (*see page 56*)

Chuleta: chop or cutlet

Churros: small fritters traditionally served for breakfast

Comino: cumin. Brought to Spain by the Moors, this spice is appreciated especially in southern Spain for its unmistakable tangy taste. Cumin is available as whole seeds or powdered.

Cream sherry: full-bodied, sweet and heavy dessert wine

Dulce: sweetmeat

Ensalada: salad, usually simply dressed with olive oil and sherry vinegar

Espinacas: spinach, traditionally served in Spain with raisins and pine-nuts

Estofado: stew

Fabada: white bean and pork stew, the most famous version of which comes from Asturias

Fino: dry sherry, light and pale yellow in colour. Serve chilled as an aperitif or to accompany an appetizer.

Fresa: strawberry. The first strawberries grown in the Huelva area appear on the market as early as mid-February.

Frito, frita: fried. In Spain, most frying is done with olive oil.

Fruta: fruit. Spain boasts a great variety of fresh fruit; more exotic varieties such as bananas and pineapples grow in the Canary Islands.

Gambas: prawns

Garbanzo: chick-pea, a popular pulse used in stews and salads

Gazpacho: Cold, refreshing vegetable soup, popular in the summer months; the tomato-and-garlic version from Andalucía is the best known.

Granada: pomegranate. If the fruit is fresh, the chewy seeds are good enough to eat. Pulp and juice are added to fruit salads, or used to make drinks or sorbets.

Helado: ice cream

Hígado: liver

Higo: fig. Fresh or dried figs are often served with ham, and are also popular as a dessert.

Al horno: baked or roasted in the oven

Huevos: eggs

Jabalí: wild boar. A popular form of game, wild boar is usually served in a stew; it is particularly delicious with figs.

Jabugo: air-dried *serrano* ham from the Andalucían highlands.

Jamón: ham

Al jerez: cooked with sherry

Jerez de la Frontera: the city in Andalucía where sherry is produced. In Spain, sherry is known as *vino de Jerez* (*see page 117*).

Judía: bean. All shapes and colours of beans are used in a variety of dishes, more often dried than fresh.

Leche: milk. Spain's dairy industry is centred on the Picos de Europa, the picturesque inland mountain range that extends into the regions of Asturias and Cantabria.

Lengua: tongue. Lamb's, pig's, calf's and ox tongue are equally popular and prepared in a variety of ways.

Lentejas: lentils. Spain is one of the leading producers of this pulse, cultivated worldwide. Lentils are nourishing and easy to digest, and much used by Spaniards in dishes such as stews.

Limón: lemon (*see page 85*)

Málaga: sweet dessert wine

Manchego: ewe's milk cheese from La Mancha (*see page 75*)

Manzana: apple; popular also in cooked dishes, for example with poultry

Manzanilla: extremely dry sherry produced in the town of Sanlúcar de Barrameda. Its unique salty flavour is due to the proximity of the vineyards to the Atlantic Ocean.

Marinade: a seasoning mixture to coat or soak meat or fish before cooking in order to tenderize or impart flavour. A wet marinade is usually made from oil, herbs, vegetables and seasoning mixed with wine, vinegar or lemon juice; a dry marinade consists of a mixture of salt, herbs and spices.

A la marinera: food cooked in a white wine sauce

Mariscos: seafood

Mejillones: mussels

Melocotón: peach. Peaches in red wine are a favourite Spanish dessert.

Melón: melon. One of Spain's favourite fruits—although it is actually a vegetable.

Membrillo: quince

Menta: mint. The finely chopped leaves of this tangy herb add flavour to sauces, salads, and vegetables.

Merluza: hake. Popular in northern Spain and Portugal, the hake is related to the cod, and has delicate white flesh. It is often sold in steaks and is used in stews.

Morcilla: Spanish air-dried blood sausage similar to black pudding. Good fried served as *tapas*, and added to stews.

Naranjas: oranges. Cultivated mainly in the huge orange groves around Valencia and Seville, oranges are used in both sweet and savoury dishes in Spain.

Oloroso: rich, strong dessert sherry, varying in colour from deep gold to brown

Paella: Spain's most famous rice dish, a colourful combination of meat, seafood, vegetables and rice cooked together and served in a large, two-handled pan.

Pan: bread

Patatas: potatoes. The Spanish national passion, often fried or made into *tortilla de patatas*—potato omelette.

Pato: duck

Pavo: turkey

Perejil: parsley. Spanish cooks prefer the flat-leaf variety, which has a rather milder flavour than the crinkly type.

Pescado: fish. Spain, surrounded on three sides by the sea, is renowned for its great variety of fish dishes.

Pichón: pigeon

Pimentón: paprika, available in mild to very hot versions. Hot paprika is used sparingly, because although Spanish food is strongly seasoned it is not over-poweringly hot.

Pimienta: pepper (from peppercorns)

Pimiento: sweet red or green pepper

Piña: pineapple

Pincho: kebab. Meat kebabs, usually made with lamb or pork, are a popular barbecue food.

Plancha: grill or griddle

A la plancha: cooked on a hot, oiled griddle. In Spanish cuisine, fish, seafood and meat can all be cooked this way.

Plátano: banana

Pollo: chicken

Pulpo: octopus

Queso: cheese. Spain has many fine cheeses, a number of which are served as appetizers.

Ragout: a well-seasoned stew of meat, poultry or fish

Rape: monkfish or angler fish; a firm, delicately flavoured fish found in the northern coastal areas of Asturias and Cantabria

Render: to refine, or melt, the pure fat out of meat or poultry fat and tissues. Rendered fat, especially pork or goose, is used for cooking.

Riñones: kidneys. Usually prepared in a sherry sauce and served as a first or main course.

Romero: rosemary. This herb grows wild in many parts of Spain, and is used generously to season fish dishes

Sal: salt

Salmón: salmon. The wild mountain rivers of the Basque Country and Navarre are full of salmon, whose flesh is firmer and leaner than farm-bred specimens

Salsa: sauce

Salt cod: *see bacalao*

Sangría: red wine punch. To make, slice 1 unwaxed lemon, 1 unwaxed orange and 1 peach, and place in a jug. Sprinkle the fruit with 60 g sugar. Add 1 litre Spanish red wine. Chill well, then add ½ litre sparkling mineral water and ice. Serve immediately.

Serrano: cured ham similar to Italian prosciutto (*see page 108*)

Seville orange: bitter orange, often used to make marmalade

Sidra: sparkling cider, a speciality of Asturias in northern Spain, where it is used in cooking and often replaces wine with a meal

Sobrasada: soft pork sausage from Majorca, similar to *chorizo* and often used as a spread

Sopa: soup. Hot and cold soups play an important role in Spanish cuisine; each region has its traditional recipes.

Tapas: appetizers—usually a mixed selection is served

Tocino: bacon

Tocino del cielo: "Little bit of heaven", Andalucían dessert made from sugar and egg yolks

Tomillo: thyme. Together with parsley and rosemary, thyme is one of the most widely used herbs in Spanish cookery. It is an essential ingredient of many lamb and game dishes.

Torta: cake or tart

Tortilla: omelette. One of the mainstays of Spanish cuisine, endlessly varied and served hot, warm or cold.

Trevélez: hard, air-dried *serrano* ham, named after the town of the same name in the Sierra Nevada

Trucha: trout. The mountain rivers of the Basque Country and Navarre produce particularly fine trout.

Truss: to secure the wings and legs of a bird against the body. This can be done by tying or sewing them with cotton or kitchen twine. The wings may also be tucked back under the bird.

Turrón: celebrated nougat from Jijona

Vieiras: scallops; a Galician speciality, usually prepared with garlic, parsley and breadcrumbs

Vinagre: vinegar. Sherry vinegar is very popular in Spain. Highly acidic, it should be used only sparingly; red wine vinegar can be used instead.

Yemas: candied egg yolks, a rich dessert created centuries ago by nuns in the bakeries of Andalucían convents

Zanahoria: carrot

Zarzuela: seafood stew from Catalonia, named after *zarzuela*, a traditional Spanish style of operetta.

CONVERSION CHART

These figures are not exact equivalents, but have been rounded up or down slightly to make measuring easier.

Weight Equivalents

Metric	Imperial
15 g	½ oz
30 g	1 oz
60 g	2 oz
90 g	3 oz
125 g	¼ lb
150 g	5 oz
200 g	7 oz
250 g	½ lb
350 g	¾ lb
500 g	1 lb
1 kg	2 to 2¼ lb

Volume Equivalents

Metric	Imperial
8 cl	3 fl oz
12.5 cl	4 fl oz
15 cl	¼ pint
17.5 cl	6 fl oz
25 cl	8 fl oz
30 cl	½ pint
35 cl	12 fl oz
45 cl	¾ pint
50 cl	16 fl oz
60 cl	1 pint
1 litre	35 fl oz

Cover: A varied selection of appetizers and generous glasses of Manzanilla sherry await guests at a *tapas* party. On offer are Moorish-style pork fillet kebabs (*page 39*), air-dried chorizo sausages, green and black olives, pearl onions in sherry vinegar (*page 33*), marinated anchovies (*page 47*) and marinated sweet red peppers (*page 34*), accompanied by crusty white bread.

TIME-LIFE BOOKS

COOKERY AROUND THE WORLD
English edition staff for *Spain*
Editorial: Ilse Gray, Luci Collings, Tim Cooke
Design: Paul Reeves
Editorial Production: Emma Wishart, Theresa John
Technical Consultant: Michael A. Barnes

English translation by Isabel Varea for Ros Schwartz Translations, London

Published originally under the title *Küchen der Welt: Spanien* by Gräfe und Unzer Verlag GmbH, Munich
© 1993 Gräfe und Unzer Verlag GmbH, Munich

This edition published by Time-Life Books B.V. Amsterdam
Authorized English language edition
© 1994 Time-Life Books B.V.
First English language printing 1994

TIME-LIFE is a trademark of Time Warner Inc. U.S.A.

ISBN 0 7054 1198 2

Colour reproduction by Fotolito Longo, Bolzano, Italy
Typeset by A. J. Latham Limited, Dunstable, Bedfordshire, England
Printed and bound by Mondadori, Verona, Italy

GRÄFE UND UNZER

EDITORS: Dr. Stephanie von Werz-Kovacs and Birgit Rademacker
Sub-Editor: Angela Hermann
Designer: Konstantin Kern
Recipes tested by: Renate Neis, Marianne Stadler
Production: Esta Denroche
Cartography: Huber, Munich
Colour Illustrations: Bengt Fosshag

Cornelia Rosales de Molino, the author, was born in Jerez de la Frontera, sherry capital of Spain, and even as a child enjoyed spending time in the kitchen. Now a food journalist living in Madrid, she is the author of several cookbooks. For this book, she has chosen only authentic Spanish recipes.

Foodphotography Eising Pete A. Eising and Susanne Eising specialize in food and drink photography and work closely with a food photographic agency operating in Germany and Switzerland. As well as cookery publishers, their clients include advertising agencies, industrial companies, newspapers and magazines. The food and props stylist responsible for this volume was Martina Görlach.

Bengt Fosshag studied graphic design in Offenbach, Germany. Since 1983 he has worked as a freelance illustrator in a wide variety of styles and subjects and the illustrations for this book stem from frequent visits to Spain over a period of more than 30 years.

Picture Credits

All photographs by Foodphotography Eising unless indicated below.

Cover: Graham Kirk, London. 4, top (2) and left, below centre (market stall, Cadaqués, Costa Brava; castle, Sierra Nevada; traditional dress, Jerez de la Frontera *feria*): Gregor M. Schmid, Gilching, by Munich. 4, left, above centre and bottom left (Corralejo beach, Fuerteventura; coastal mountains, Tenerife): Thomas Stankiewicz, Munich. 4, bottom right (Sitges wine festival): Martin Thomas, Aachen. 5, top (wrought iron balconies, Seville): Thomas Stankiewicz, Munich. 5, centre (La Giralda, Seville): Gregor M. Schmid, Gilching, near Munich. 5, bottom (Ampurias, near L'Escala, Costa Brava): Martin Thomas, Aachen. 8/9: Thomas Stankiewicz, Munich. 10, 11: B. Barajas, Bildagentur J.D., Munich. 12, top: Thomas Stankiewicz, Munich. 12, bottom: Spanish Tourist Office. 13, 14 (2): Martin Thomas, Aachen. 15: Thomas Stankiewicz, Munich. 16, top: Spanish Tourist Office. 16, bottom and 16/17: Werner Neumeister, Munich. 18: Martin Thomas, Munich. 19 (2): Armin Faber, Mühlheim. 20, top and 21, bottom: Thomas Stankiewicz, Munich. 20, bottom and 21, top: A. M. Gross, Bildagentur J.D., Munich. 22: Spanish Tourist Office. 23: A. M. Gross, Bildagentur J.D., Munich. 24/25: real bild, Klaus D. Neumann, Munich. 25 (2): Spanish Tourist Office. 26: Gregor M. Schmid, Gilching, near Munich. 27 (2), 29 (2): Thomas Stankiewicz, Munich. 28, top: Thomas Widmann, Regensburg. 28, bottom: Martin Thomas, Aachen. 50: A. M. Gross, Bildagentur J.D., Munich. 71: Fotostudio Teubner, Füssen-Horn. 85: ai aigner impuls, Gottfried Aigner, Munich. 128: real bild, Klaus D. Neumann, Munich.